Men Navigating Midlife

Robyn Vickers-Willis

Men Navigating Midlife
By Robyn Vickers-Willis
Allen &Unwin
Publication: September 2004
$16.95, paper, 5 ½ x 8, 288 pages
ISBN 1741142679
Publicity contact: Catherine Bosin
Independent Publishers Group
(312) 337-0747; cbosin@ipgbook.com

ALLEN&UNWIN

Dedicated to all the men who contributed to
Men Navigating Midlife

The author would like to thank Collins Publishers for their permission to use
the poem from Michael Leunig's *Common Prayer Collection*.

Myers-Briggs Type Indicator and MBTI are registered trademarks
of Consulting Psychologists Press, Inc.

First published in 2004
Copyright © Robyn Vickers-Willis 2004

Allen & Unwin
83 Alexander Street,
Crows Nest NSW 2065 Australia
Phone: (61 2) 8425 0100
Fax: (61 2) 9906 2218
E-mail: info@allenandunwin.com
Web: www.allenandunwin.com

National Library of Australia
Cataloguing-in-Publication entry:

Vickers-Willis, Robyn, 1952– .
Men navigating midlife.

Bibliography.
Includes index.
ISBN 1 74114 267 9.

1. Middle aged men. 2. Middle aged men – Life skills
guides. 3. Middle age – Psychological aspects. I. Title.

305.2441

Set in 11/14 pt Adobe Garamond by Midland Typesetters, Maryborough, Victoria
Printed by McPherson's Printing Group

10 9 8 7 6 5 4 3 2 1

foreword

MIDLIFE IN ITS MANY dimensions is a blank spot in our culture. Yet never before has our world been more in need of the wisdom that comes from those who are willing to go on the profound psychological and spiritual journey that occurs at midlife.

We are fortunate indeed that Robyn Vickers-Willis has once again brought midlife transition vibrantly to life as she continues to demonstrate her insight and sensitivity for this often misunderstood, highly significant stage. Through storytelling, personal reflections and the use of metaphor she explores this heroic journey towards wholeness, balance and the wisdom of the elder. In *Men Navigating Midlife* she presents the candid and compelling personal stories of the men she interviewed. Sharing her own experiences and insights, Robyn provides practical exercises while exploring the themes that emerge from these men's stories.

Men Navigating Midlife is a valuable contribution to our understanding about midlife transition and a companion piece to Robyn Vickers-Willis' first book, *Navigating Midlife: women becoming themselves*. Her writing is warm, direct and accessible. Whether you are just approaching midlife, new into midlife, long into midlife, beyond midlife or just wanting to understand better this stage of life, you will find this book speaks to your mind and your heart. May it have a long publishing life.

Robert A. Johnson
Best-selling author of *He, She, We, Inner Work, Transformation, Owning Your Own Shadow* and *Balancing Heaven and Earth*

contents

preface

WHEN I WROTE MY first book about midlife transition, *Navigating Midlife: women becoming themselves*, I focused on women's experiences at midlife, deciding that my second book would be for men. Interestingly, when male friends and clients read the book they made comments such as, 'But I feel like that too' or, 'It was the same for me'. The first time I went on talkback radio to discuss *Navigating Midlife: Women becoming themselves* I had more men than women ringing in to ask questions, and whenever I have spoken about the book there have nearly always been interested men present. And often women have asked questions such as, 'Is it the same for my husband/partner/brother?' So writing *Men Navigating Midlife* feels like a natural progression for me in my writing journey.

Men Navigating Midlife is a book about men, written for both men and women. In my first book, my own story and the stories of other women provided the vehicle to explore strategies and understandings that assist the process of midlife transition. In this book, men's stories have been the vehicle through which we continue our exploration of understandings and strategies that support us as we navigate midlife transition. At times these are particularly pertinent to a man's journey at midlife. However, for the most part the themes explored are just as relevant for women as they are for men.

I have been a psychologist for 25 years and during this time I have always worked with male as well as female clients. I grew up with three brothers and a father, and despite going to an all-girls' school, I have always had several platonic male friends from an early age. I was married for eighteen years and our relationship had both egalitarian and traditional qualities. I am a mother of a daughter and two sons, all born in the early 1980s. As a result of the women's movement, issues of stereotyping, of nurture versus nature, have been a fairly constant part of my personal and professional thinking life since I was a young woman.

Over the course of my life's journey, I have moved through many different stages in how I relate to men. Because of the type of young girl I was, and because of what I observed as acceptable and worthy of attention when I was young, I often wished I was a boy. This feeling stayed with me until I was in my mid-thirties. As I struggled with my own 'inner male' and started to empower myself and engage in the world in a way that better suited me, I increasingly appreciated being a woman. I also believe some resentment within me that I had projected onto men began to decline.

In the past ten years I have gradually come to a place where I feel very grateful for my life as I enjoy the friendship and companionship of a variety of men and women. I acknowledge that there are differences between us; however, increasingly I wonder how much of this is due to our conditioning, rather than innate gender differences. And after using Carl Jung's understandings around personality type while working as an organisational consultant in the past fifteen years, I now see that personality can cut across gender expectations. I believe we are each unique individuals, whether male or female, and the more we can grow into and celebrate our own uniqueness, and the uniqueness of others, the better off we are, and the better off the world will be. As we celebrate our uniqueness we become more willing to see our commonality. This understanding becomes particularly pertinent as we move through the significant psychological developmental stage of midlife transition.

For the twelve years before starting to write, I ran my own business. I was a consultant to corporations and my work involved facilitating a variety of aspects of corporate change management, including development of personnel, developing and running courses in such areas as leadership development, team development, mentoring and performance management. I also carried out individual counselling and coaching. Very early on I realised what a privileged position I was in as men shared their vulnerabilities with me—something I know men don't necessarily easily do. I had a sense that because I was a female consultant I was allowed insights that a male consultant might not be. I remember discussing this with one of my interviewees who worked in the business world. He said, 'When I am talking to a man I'm always sort of on the defensive—it's as though there is always this competition going on between us. With you, it is different. I trust that you will still think I'm okay no matter what I say.'

Once I finished *Navigating Midlife: women becoming themselves*, I started to interview men for this second book, to see what they had to say about their experience of midlife transition. Would men spontaneously come up with similar themes to those explored in my first book? Through the interview process I tried to ask questions only when I felt men needed encouragement to expand on themes they were discussing. I wanted men to tell their stories however they wished.

I interviewed over 30 men who were prepared to share aspects of their inner and outer worlds. These represent the full educational range. Some left school at fifteen years of age and have had no further formal education. Others had completed years of tertiary training; some had achieved doctoral qualifications. Some were professionals, either on a salary or self-employed; others worked in a trade; some were studying. Interviewees ranged in age from 37 years to 53 years. Some were married, others divorced, some never married, some remarried, and others were in a de facto relationship. All names have been changed. Also, while being careful not to change the psychological content of their stories, I have altered some of the background details of the interviewees so that identities are disguised. I appreciate enormously the generosity of spirit of these men as they have contributed their time, their hearts, their minds and parts of their life stories to assist me in my project.

When I mentioned this book to friends and acquaintances, often their response was, 'But can you get men to talk?' I have found that interviewees have been keen to talk and to be listened to. Men have told me that they enjoyed having the opportunity to tell their story. This did not surprise me as I already knew from researching my first book that telling your story at midlife is a healing thing to do.

Interviews usually went for one and a half hours. In the interviews several men talked about their loneliness and how they would love to be able to share with other men in the way they were with me. Few had taken the steps to find a 'safe place' where they could speak to men in such an open way. My hope is that as they read this book, men will find a place to share and better understand their own story, as well as become aware of a variety of ideas and tools they can use to support themselves as they navigate midlife.

In the process of researching this book I have read many books written by and for men. I have incorporated some of their insights along with the stories of those I interviewed and my own observations and experiences of the midlife journey. My aim has been to work sensitively as I explore the many issues facing men at midlife, to be a compassionate commentator, an attitude that has increasingly become my approach towards men over the past ten years, both in my personal and professional life.

I believe the women's movement has done much to raise the consciousness of women of the baby boomer generation so that many have been able to take full advantage of the window of opportunity for personal growth and healing at midlife. They are doing this in a way our mothers' generation was not empowered to do. All of us are affected by the limitations of living within the stereotype of a power-focused society. It often determines what parts of us we disown as we conform in the first half of our life. In such a society women have not fared well; however, neither have many men. I believe that baby boomer men in the West are themselves struggling to create liberation from the restrictiveness of living in a power-focused society.

It is normal in the first half of life to disown parts of ourselves as we conform to the society we live in. However, if we are ultimately to fulfil our destiny and contribute to society with the 'wisdom of the elder', we need to be willing to move beyond the restrictiveness of our culture's gender stereotypes. My hope is that, as men read *Men Navigating Midlife*, connect with other men's stories, connect with their own, and learn about the importance of moving through midlife transition, they find a way to create a second half of life that is alive with personal meaning.

I wish to thank a number of people—first of all, to the men who generously gave their time and parts of their life stories to *Men Navigating Midlife*. My friend Elizabeth Ackland and her daughter, Jackie, shared their beautiful home with me in the Byron Bay hinterland, as did Robert Bruce—places to which I retreated to write. Nurturing times with my friend, Siegfried Gutbrod, have supported me as I wrote. Peter Hay, Ross Johnston, Dr Manfred Krautschneider, Heather Nankervis, Ian Renard and Paul Sanders gave me support by reading the final manuscript and providing invaluable feedback. The wonderful publishing team from Allen & Unwin have once again worked with sensitivity and professionalism—Annette Barlow, the senior commissioning editor; Colette Vella, the senior editor; Karen Ward, the copyeditor; and Nada Backovic, the cover designer. As always, my children have been a constant source of love and encouragement. And finally, to all the other people in my life who have given me support along the way, thank you.

Robyn Vickers-Willis, January 2004

CHAPTER 1

introduction

Two roads diverged in a wood, and I—
I took the one less travelled by,
And that has made all the difference.

Robert Frost, 'The Road Not Taken'

I look around me at my job, my family, my home, my car, my life and none of it seems to mean anything to me anymore. The thought of sitting in another business meeting makes me feel sick to the stomach and at home I'm like a stranger to my wife and kids. The only time I feel remotely relaxed is when I'm playing computer games or watching television . . . there must be more to life than this! Joanne is nagging me and now I keep fantasising about leaving a farewell note on the kitchen table, getting in my car and just driving as far away as possible. I think I'm going crazy. You see, it's only a little while ago I thought my life was pretty perfect. (John, aged 42)

MENTION THE TERM 'male midlife crisis' and it is likely to instigate jokes and stories about flashy sports cars, young blondes and endless hours in front of the mirror. It conjures up images of men creating all sorts of distractions to stop themselves noticing that they are getting older. To use the word 'crisis' to describe a man's experience at this time of life can be destructive to his own personal growth, for by doing so a mindset can be created that this is a thing to fear, to avoid, to repress. This stereotypical way of viewing men's midlife change as a 'crisis' adds even further to men's anxiety as they feel from within a need to make significant changes in their life. For between the ages of 35 to 50 their psyche is pushing them to do the significant inner psychological work of midlife transition.

A TIME OF SIGNIFICANT PSYCHOLOGICAL CHANGE

Our psyche is pre-programmed to encourage us to make changes at certain ages in our life, give or take a few years, so that we can move on to the next developmental stage. It is like a blueprint within all of us. We acknowledge that adolescents go through a time of significant change as they move through the transition from childhood to early adulthood. From their early teens until about twenty years of age a young person's psyche encourages them to complete the tasks of separating from the ways of their childhood and to move towards being part of the adult world. There is an equally important stage of psychological transition for adults at midlife as we move from early adulthood to middle adulthood.

A key concept of psychological growth conceived by Carl Jung, the renowned Swiss psychoanalyst, is that of *individuation*. Individuation is a process within our psyche encouraging us to become more uniquely individual. If individuation goes well, gradually, over our life span we each acquire a fuller, clearer and unique identity. It is a crucial aspect of development in childhood and adolescence. Jung was the first psychologist to recognise that a resurgence of individuation occurs in the middle years and continues through the rest of life.

Midlife transition is a bridging time between the first and second half of life with the dividing period being somewhere around 40. The usual pattern of psychological development in the first half is to create a life based on what others—especially parents, other significant adults, our peers and society in general—expect of us. Therefore, up to his mid to late thirties a man normally refers to his outer world to determine how he should live. For healthy development in the second half of life we refer to our inner world to determine how we should live. To achieve this transition in life orientation at midlife we must give priority in our life to two tasks— to go within to find out more about our own true nature, and concurrently start creating a life where we can be the person we realise we are.

Turbulent feelings are normal at midlife

This transition between the first and second half of life is not like a solid bridge that we can easily stroll across. It is more like a flimsy swing bridge, seemingly over the deep chasm of the unknown. There are usually feelings of great insecurity. Some may navigate this bridge and the developmental tasks with a certain amount of ease, although from my observation this is rare. Others start across, get scared and go back, perhaps never to venture out again. Others find the first steps very scary, but once they have started they know there is no turning back. Some try to jump to the other side too quickly and in the process end up feeling very precarious and unbalanced in their life situation. They may never find a steady enough hold to cross the bridge of midlife transition.

A traumatic event frequently plays an important part in insti-gating midlife transition. The same event would have different meaning and consequences if it occurred at another time in life, for at around 40 we are not simply reacting to this external situation. We are also acting on the internal promptings from our psyche.

An event, such as divorce, ill health or the loss of his job may trigger the start of a man's reappraisal of himself and his whole life. Such an event may bring about what is commonly referred to as a 'midlife crisis'. The crisis is the actual point of choice. Will he change or won't he? He may start a period of reappraisal, or, alternatively, he may ignore the inner promptings from his psyche and choose to do little to get to know himself better. For example, during a life-threatening illness a man might realise how tired he is of pushing his way through his work to the point of exhaustion, yet returns to work and his old life as if nothing has happened.

Perhaps he is fearful of losing the identity he has maintained for so long; or that if he looks into his inner world he will find there is nothing of substance there; or that he will not like what he finds. He continues on as he has done, although others will notice a lack of spark, a resigned acceptance, a rigidity and weariness in his demeanour. He is 'battening down the hatches' to continue his journey in the second half of life in more or less the same way as he has in the first.

Or after an event such as a marriage breakdown a man may make dramatic external changes, flipping from one extreme lifestyle to another, such as from a conservative, restrictive lifestyle to a permissive one. If he continues on this path without taking the time to get to know himself, he is likely to be no more in touch with his true self in the second half of life than he was in the first. In both these cases a man is avoiding the long and at times arduous journey of midlife transition. He also relinquishes the opportunity of enjoying the benefits of this journey—a second half of life full of personal meaning, vitality, joy and passion.

How will you know if you have started midlife transition? Perhaps you will experience one of the situations just described, which might set you on a path of ongoing reflection and transformation. Or perhaps somewhere around the age of 40 you will start feeling a discontent. You no longer feel fired up about the work to which you have so eagerly given lots of time and energy in the past. Much of your life feels meaningless to you. Your energy is low. These feelings are encouraging you to reappraise who you are and how you are living your life.

TIME ALONE FOR SELF-REFLECTION IS ESSENTIAL AT MIDLIFE

If you ignore these feelings, through busyness or diversions such as affairs, alcohol or endless acquisition, your body sends even stronger signs. You feel depressed. You become snappy with your family, friends and colleagues. You might experience a debilitating illness. All these are warning signs for you to stop, to go within and take the time to ask yourself the following questions.

- Who am I?
- How contented am I with my life—my work, my relationships, my leisure time?
- Given that I am halfway through my life, do I want to keep on living my life in the same way or do I want to make changes?
- What is meaningful to me?
- What do I value? Is my life reflecting these values?
- By what beliefs have I been living my life? Whose are they? Are they just illusions?
- What could I do to start tapping into unknown parts of myself?
- What stops me from making changes?

The way men respond to the challenge of finding answers to these questions depends on a variety of factors—their personality, their past experiences, perceived flexibility within their present life structure, and how effectively they have completed the tasks of past developmental stages. Some will quickly take on the challenge of this inner questioning, finding a variety of ways to explore themselves and their world. Others will go very slowly and cautiously, making changes after much careful analysis. Some will be terrified at the thought of changing anything and will hold on to their old life in fear. They may make superficial changes in their outer life, but never truly come to grips with who they are—still choosing to live by society's expectations of them, rather than looking within themselves for their own answers. Other men will find superficial answers to these questions, not wanting to do the hard, soul-searching work of midlife transition, and as a result create a different, but equally incongruent lifestyle.

FINDING ANSWERS TO MIDLIFE QUESTIONS

So how do men start finding answers to some of these questions? Do men and women navigate midlife transition in similar ways or are there significant differences in how they experience this stage of life? Each person's story is unique; no other person's process of growth and change is exactly like our own. Nevertheless, others' stories can serve as a guide in contacting our own inner wisdom by showing us a way inside ourself to where the voice most important to us dwells. When we find that voice, we must treasure it, as it will help us to navigate the journey of midlife transition to our own true identity in the second half of life. My intent is that *Men Navigating Midlife* offers a framework for exploring and understanding men's midlife journey to that inner wisdom.

THE BENEFITS ARE ENORMOUS

Moving through midlife transition often involves much pain. So why choose to move through it? What has a man to gain from this journey? As I describe some of the benefits of midlife transition, ask yourself how it would be to have them as part of your life.

A man who has moved through midlife transition has passion for what he is doing because it is deeply connected to what is most meaningful to him. His body is relaxed. He is vital. He has a sparkle in his eyes. He has a deep understanding and connection with himself, and at the same time is able to connect with ease and under-standing to others. He is tolerant, not extreme in his views, and balanced in how he approaches and judges himself and others.

The world he has created for himself in the second half of his life suits him well, so his journey often seems easier than it did in the first half of life. He is free of addictions. By this I do not mean he won't enjoy a drink from time to time, or whatever takes his fancy. However, when he does, it is out of pure pleasure, not as a way of running away from his pain. He is comfortable not only with experiencing his feelings, but also with talking about them. This in turn allows him to develop relationships with others that are open and that acknowledge everyone's needs and interests. He has an expanded ability to nourish and honour all parts of himself—his physical, emotional, intellectual and spiritual selves. He also has an expanded ability to nourish others. With increased awareness of who he is and what is important to him, he develops intimate and honest relationships with himself, with others, and with his environment. And with this increased awareness he is also able to own and honour his unique abilities and wisdom, and share them in the world.

I hope this description is enough to encourage you to read on, for as you can see the benefits of moving through midlife transition are enormous!

PART 1

What is midlife transition?

the psychology of
midlife transition

God bless our contradictions, those parts of us which seem out of character.
Let us be boldly and gladly out of character. Let us be creatures of paradox
and variety; creators of contrast; of light and shade; creatures of faith.
God be our constant. Let us step out of character into the unknown,
to struggle and love and do what we will. Amen

Michael Leunig, *Common Prayer Collection*

WHILE WRITING MY FIRST book on midlife at the age of 47
I read over 100 books, mainly psychological ones, and many based
on the teachings of Carl Jung, the renowned Swiss psychoanalyst. My
reading and writing helped me to understand and then conceptualise
my own experience of midlife transition.

It wasn't until after I had completed my six years of training to be
a psychologist and counsellor that I learnt a lot about Jung's ideas.
Some psychologists are wary of them. One of the reasons is because
of his spiritual, as well as psychological focus. Yet for me this is an
important aspect of his work. As we live in a materialistic world and
struggle to have spirituality as part of our lives, Jung's ideas can show
us how to bridge the two and create meaning in our lives.

Jung's psychology is a 'meaning making' psychology. From within the Jungian framework meaning is found when we connect with our inner world through activities such as making time to just 'be', analysing our dreams, writing in a journal, exploring myths and fairy tales, engaging in music, dance and a variety of other creative pursuits. For Jung, the unconscious is the source of creativity in our lives. At midlife we can use his ideas to release within ourselves a creative way of living and of being that in the past has seemed like an impossible dream. Jung's ideas are many and varied. As we read about them and discover that they resonate with our own life and with what we observe in others, we find his ideas are also meaningful and useful. His theories link in with belief systems of many other cultures. He developed his ideas first, and then discovered these links and saw this as affirmation of his understandings.

If Jung's psychology is of no interest to you, you can skip this chapter and still benefit from the rest of the book. However, while researching and speaking on midlife I have become aware that he has a wide following. His psychological insights have much to offer us today as we all search for how to create meaning in our own lives at a time when our larger world increasingly seems to lack it. If you have not read of his ideas before, I suggest you suspend judgment, and read on.

THE PSYCHE

Jung called our total psychological structure the *psyche,* the Greek word for soul. He conceived the psyche as having three layers of consciousness. At the surface is the *conscious,* below this is the *personal unconscious*, and at the base the *collective unconscious.* We can compare it to an iceberg. The top layer, the conscious, is that part that can be seen. The middle layer, the personal unconscious, is just below the surface of awareness. We most easily become aware of its contents when we are willing to dive below the surface. The bottom layer, the collective unconscious, is way down deep and is by far the biggest part. As when the *Titanic* hit the iceberg, it is the part below the surface that we can't see and are not aware of that can most easily sink us.

The conscious contains all those psychological parts of ourselves we are aware of and can control and direct at will. When we are living consciously we are adaptable, flexible, discerning and rational and we evaluate ourself and others in non-extreme ways. We view life in shades of grey, rather than in black and white. In the first half of life our conscious feels big and busy, but is in fact the part of our psyche that least directs our behaviour. Until we have moved through midlife transition much of our behaviour is dominated by our unconscious.

Our personal unconscious is made up of our unwanted desires, uncivilised impulses and forbidden feelings and beliefs that we have repressed from consciousness, deliberately or unconsciously forgotten. Here we also find hidden positive and creative qualities and abilities. Our collective unconscious is the part of our unconscious that is not individual, but rather universal and shared. It contains the archetypes.

Archetypes are deep and abiding patterns of being, behaving, perceiving and responding. They remain powerful and present in all of us over time, although they need to be activated within us for us to experience them. They are found in the archetypal stories and mythology of all peoples and are responsible for universal tendencies occurring throughout humankind. For example, when activated in a positive way, the warrior archetype helps us to claim our power and assert our identity in the world. Major archetypal images that are important in understanding psychic processes at midlife are the *persona*, the *shadow* and the *Self*.

THE DEVELOPMENT OF THE EGO AND THE PERSONA

We experience a number of transitions in the first half of life and they all help us to become a separate social identity. Up until the age of about fourteen years much of what we do psychologically is governed by instinct, by our unconscious. Around puberty consciousness really begins to develop. From this time until midlife we transform our nature by developing a strong *ego* and *persona*.

The ego is made up of those parts we are prepared to accept as ourself. From this conscious understanding about who we are, we create various personae, or masks. We make our choice about which personae to show depending on what we see as acceptable or as being required by different people and situations in our life. If all goes well in our development in the first half of life, we transform our true nature into a strong ego and persona. We develop our strengths and this inevitably leads to one-sidedness in our nature. We find ways of supporting ourselves emotionally and physically by developing effective relationships, interests and careers. This is what is required to create a solid foundation for our self in the first half of life. In the first half of life it is very much an outer journey and it's very important that it be so, as we need to create a place where we can feel secure in the world. In Jungian psychology it is critical to develop a strong ego in the first half of life if we are to navigate midlife transition.

PSYCHIC ENERGY

Energy operating in the psyche, known as *psychic energy,* moves in a direction so as to maintain balance, or to compensate, within our psyche. In the first half of life, every affirmation that we have made in the conscious mind has had its opposite affirmed in the unconscious. For every wish and every intention that we are aware of, we also unconsciously wish and intend the opposite. And the differentiation of our conscious affirmations from our unconscious opposites actually creates the psychic energy, also known as *libido*, that runs our psyche. For example, if you grew up with an overly controlling attitude to your outer, conscious world your psychic energy would counterbalance this attitude by presenting a compensating 'out of control' attitude in your inner, unconscious world.

The Shadow

As more favourable or socially acceptable parts of our self are intensified in our conscious, their opposites are pushed back into our unconscious. This weaker side coalesces into our *shadow*. These shadow aspects in ourselves are often projected onto others in whom they may or may not be present. Our shadow also shows itself in unaccountable behaviour where we find ourselves saying, 'I was not myself. I don't know what came over me.'

The Self

At midlife our psyche encourages us to take an inner journey to integrate the contents of our unconscious, bring together all the missing parts of ourself, including our shadow, into a complete and whole conscious *Self.* This Self in Jungian psychology is the centre of our being, both conscious and unconscious. It is distinct from our ego, which is the centre of our conscious life. This Self is in contrast to the self used in everyday terminology. When I use Self in this book, with a capital S, I am referring to that which represents our truest nature.

Individuation

The process of moving towards wholeness is known in Jungian psychology as *individuation*. The Self archetype is the prime mover in our psyche at midlife moving us towards individuation. Individuation occurs all our life, however it is at its most potent at midlife. From around 35 years of age, our Self encourages us to reclaim all those parts of ourselves that we repressed in our unconscious in the process of conforming in the first half of life, as well as other parts we have never been conscious of. As we do this work and become more of the person we were born to be, we create more balance in our psyche and greater psychological health.

BALANCE AND PSYCHOLOGICAL HEALTH

In Jungian theory psychological health is defined as balance between all of the opposite attitudes, desires and ways of being that are part of us. As we allow ourselves to move through the process of individuation, we find ways to bring about the integration of these opposites. As we become more aware of these opposites within us, it is important for us to live creatively so we can accept and express every part of ourselves. For example, when we have lived a very structured first half of life, it is important to find creative ways to live more flexibly. This way we are able to draw on both our structured and flexible attitudes, integrating these polarities. This leads to increased balance and psychological health.

MIDLIFE TRANSITION

Somewhere between the ages of 35 to 40 there is a shift within our psyche as our ego loses energy. This encourages the contents from our unconscious to come up to consciousness. This change can be a gradual process experienced as a growing realisation that we aren't the person we thought we were. Roles and relationships with our work and with intimate others start to feel restrictive. With increasing incongruence between the person inside we now perceive, and the life we are living, we feel desperate to make a change.

Often midlife transition is instigated through a traumatic happening, such as loss of parents, marriage breakdown, loss of job or loss of health. Such a traumatic happening has a different impact on us at midlife to other times of life. With our ego weakening, such an event encourages us to question all the values, attitudes and assumptions that have given us meaning and certainty in the first half of life. It is as though our sense of who we are and what we want in our life collapses along with all our attitudes, beliefs and illusions.

This is a time of great confusion as much of our suppressed unconscious comes to the surface. For example, if previously we felt in control, now we feel out of control. If we have been strong our vulnerability will now overwhelm us. If we have experienced our first half of life primarily through words, now words will fail us. If our feelings were suppressed and we approached life in a passionless way, now our feelings overwhelm us. If we have been weak we will now express strength. If we have been energetic, we will now be languid. If we have been very close in our relationships, we will now yearn for separateness. If we have been alone, we will now yearn for connection.

THE THREE STAGES OF MIDLIFE TRANSITION

Whether change starts traumatically or as a slower process, we move through three distinct phases in midlife transition. In his book, *In Midlife*, Murray Stein describes these three stages as *separation*, *liminality* and *reintegration*. Although these stages will be discussed in a discrete, linear way they are from my experience a more flowing and at times chaotically interwoven process.

SEPARATION

At the beginning of midlife transition, without necessarily knowing why we are doing so, we find ourselves observing our personae, the masks we have developed in the first half of life. The word 'persona' comes from the Latin word for mask and actors wore them on the ancient stage. During the first half of life we develop these personae, or masks, to help us adapt to the various situations and people we deal with. For example, a man might present an easygoing, chatty persona with friends and a reserved and analytical persona with colleagues. His various masks become his conscious idea of himself and in all their different forms become his ego. To achieve separation, the first stage of midlife transition, a man has to separate his under-standing of Self from these masks. Perhaps an example will help here.

Bob

I met Bob, aged 49, a couple of years ago. He had just moved from the family property in country Victoria to the city, after working the land and raising a family there for twenty years. When I met him he was in his second year of studying social work with the goal to work with young people. I was fascinated to hear more about Bob's story, recognising what a huge shift he and his family had made. He talked about how in his late thirties he almost overnight sensed a lack of energy for the work he had so easily done before. Until that time there had never been any doubt that he would work the land all his life. He told me, 'Being the only son, I was expected to come home to the farm. I had never questioned this assumption.'

Over the next couple of years, despite good seasons, his income decreased as he stopped being so attentive to the myriad of things he needed to do. He described how anxious he became; he wondered if he was going crazy. From being a hardworking, focused, confident farmer, husband and father he had become an unreliable, anxious, depressed person. After several months of just hoping everything would get back to 'normal' he was galvanized into action when a local farmer suicided. Finally acknowledging to himself how bad he was feeling, he consulted his general practitioner who referred him to a local counsellor. After several months of weekly counselling he started to accept that he had a yearning to leave the country life and move back to the city where he had studied agricultural science many years beforehand. At this stage he wasn't clear what he wanted to do there, he just knew he wanted to make the change. At first his wife was resistant, but then accepted that with their two daughters about to move to the city for further study, it might work. She also began to realise that she could more easily start fulfilling some of her own dreams by accessing many of the advantages of living in a city.

In his book, *In Midlife*, Stein talks about a 'crack' opening in our identity, a crack that appears between the person we have appeared to be in our own eyes and in the eyes of others, and the person we are now starting to sense we truly are. He goes on to say that as terrifying as the experience of this sudden 'crack' in the identity is, it is often the best way, for otherwise the ego's natural defences will pull the persona back into place, even though it will now appear a little false. So a man may experience the crack and be so terrified at the thought of leaving his persona identification behind that he pretends nothing has happened and continues living as he has in the past, although a psychological 'unease' can be detected in 'increasingly rigid, out-moded and anxious behaviour'. An extreme example of this is when after a man loses his job, he is unable to tell his wife, and still dresses for work each morning, leaving the house and pretending he still has a job.

Bob explained how distressed he felt as so many of the dreams and ideals he had held about himself and his life disappeared. He often felt overwhelmed by negative feelings and thoughts and wondered if he was going crazy. Having no understanding of why he was feeling as he was he at times felt suicidal, and even planned how to do it. Once he started counselling he found the support he needed to grieve, mourn and then let go of roles, attitudes, values and ways of being that he now knew were not congruent with the person he was starting to recognise he was.

At separation it is normal for a man to experience a range of intense emotions. He may feel grief about dreams that haven't been realised; fear about his feelings that can be overwhelming; and disillusionment with his present life. These emotions can lead to physical and emotional exhaustion. During this time a man supports himself by creating time for reflection, talking to loved ones, coun-selling, journal writing and any other activity that allows him to be present to himself and his feelings.

If a man is unable to find support for himself at this stage his feelings may easily overwhelm him, perhaps even lead to thoughts of suicide. If he has these thoughts it is vital that he gets professional help. If he becomes overwrought, antidepressants may be necessary.

He needs to be reassured that what he is experiencing is normal given his stage of life, and that he needs to find some support, both professional and otherwise, where he feels safe to explore and express his innermost feelings and thoughts.

At separation much of a man's psychic energy will be directed to:

- separating his own values from those he has acquired during the first half of life
- learning how to connect with and express his emotions
- developing an increased awareness of his personae, or masks, and determining which are part of his authentic Self and which he wants to discard
- grieving for dreams that won't be realised
- forgiving himself and others
- finding a balance between this grieving and moving forward
- becoming aware of new possibilities for his life.

LIMINALITY

Once a man starts separating from his old way of life, even if it is just psychological separation rather than physical separation, he moves on to the second stage of midlife transition. Liminality is seen as the central experience of the midlife journey. In Latin, *limen* means threshold or doorway, a space betwixt and between. There are strong feelings of confusion, bewilderment and disorientation at this time as a man lets go of his old understanding of himself and the life he wants to live and floats towards the as yet unrealised Self and future. Bob described how he experienced extreme lethargy and then anxiety as he felt 'all at sea' over a period of several years when he gradually let go of all the ways he had defined himself and his world without as yet knowing how things would unfold for him and his family.

In liminality a man has made the decision to leave behind his old identity and old life but is as yet very unsure about the new life he is to create for himself. Often, he can find this time terrifying. Doubts creep in about whether he has the resources to manage and whether it is just easier to return to the old way of being. It is normal to feel pulled back to the familiar, as with old ways of defining himself and his world gone, a man no longer feels secure. It is important that he gather around himself the support of loved ones, friends and others to sustain him during this uncertain time. Some self-imposed daily routine and structure can also help, as so much else is changing. Bob described how after talking to his counsellor he was prompted to write in a journal every day for half an hour and to go for long afternoon walks. As well as giving some structure to his day, an added bonus of these activities was that they helped him to start finding answers to the myriad of questions running through his mind.

Some helpful questions we can ask ourselves when we feel we are in the liminality stage are:

- If I am not the person I thought I was, who am I?
- Now that I have decided to make a change, how do I want to live my life from here onwards? What are my dreams, daydreams and fantasies trying to tell me?
- What's important to me? What do I want to make time for? What are my values?
- How can I best support myself as I go through all this change?

REINTEGRATION

During the third phase of midlife transition, reintegration, a man moves into the second half of life. After much soul-searching he starts making decisions that enable him to start creating a life that reflects his understanding of Self. Bob finally committed to studying social work and three years later, plans now to dedicate his time to working with young people. After much hard work, life is starting to feel easier as he gains confidence in himself and his new life. He agrees that he still has times when he feels 'all at sea'; however, this usually only lasts for a couple of days, or at the most a couple of weeks.

During these times he writes in his journal and talks to one friend in particular who is doing the same course. He has also rediscovered his love of music and uses this to relax. He accepts that these 'all at sea' feelings are just part of his stretching of boundaries. Bob also mentioned that a side benefit of all these changes is that as he has become more in touch with himself, his relationship with his daughters has deepened.

As we achieve the third stage of midlife transition, reintegration, we accept that we have an inner guiding system which helps us to decide how we should live. No longer do we define ourselves or our life by the expectations of our outer world. As we find ways to connect with our inner world we naturally find ourselves:

- reassessing our life goals
- increasing our vigilance about living consciously through daily reflection to check that we are not slipping back into ego-based rather than Self-based decisions
- continuing to integrate our opposites—the repressed attitudes and desires that are part of us
- remaining open to ongoing change and development
- developing increased congruence in all aspects of our life
- enjoying living creatively.

Once we have moved through these three stages of midlife transition others perceive us as natural, open, centred, authentic, accepting and joyous. We will be aware of an ease within our self and a passion for life that can seem quite miraculous. This does not mean that life is easy. As we continue to learn more about ourselves we continue to make changes in our life and in our perception of our Self. This growth comes from being willing to go through the difficult times—and as time goes on we become increasingly confident in our Self-knowledge and skills to deal with the storms and backwaters as we navigate our life.

CHAPTER 3

a hero's journey

The hero comes back from this mysterious adventure
with the power to bestow boons on his fellow man.

Joseph Campbell, *The Hero With a Thousand Faces*

IN HIS CLASSIC STUDY OF world mythology, *The Hero With a Thousand Faces*, Joseph Campbell found in the mythology of virtually all cultures stories about a quest for meaning and transformation during adulthood—a time when men and women go on a journey, confront their own dragons, and return with the treasure of their true selves. At journey's end, there is the reward of a sense of true connection with oneself, with others, and with the world at large, and an understanding of one's destiny; all enabling the hero to bestow boons on his fellow man.

Campbell's description of a hero's journey is that first the hero becomes restless as he senses there is something missing in his life and, second, he embarks on a journey, an adventure, to search for these missing parts. A man's midlife journey can be viewed in a similar way. At midlife he senses there is something lacking, and so he goes on a journey of discovery. At first he may search outside himself—a new partner, a new job, a new car—however, the feelings will persist until he starts to go on a journey to his inner world. And what he is looking for are repressed parts of himself, for it is these he needs to integrate into himself if he is to move towards individuation, one of the main tasks of midlife transition.

RECLAIMING REPRESSED PARTS OF OURSELF

Individuation is taking place all our life, but it is at its most potent at midlife. At midlife our psychic energy is encouraging us to become complete, to become whole. An individuated person has fully developed all parts of themself—their intellectual, physical, emotional and spiritual selves. No person is ever fully individuated; however, midlife transition is the time of the greatest opportunity to realise, to make conscious much of our potential. To do this, our greatest task is to bring to consciousness repressed and never-known parts of ourself. As we do this work we start experiencing a much greater range of feelings and thoughts, a greater energy and zest for life, and a more tolerant and balanced attitude towards ourself and others.

Why do parts of us get repressed in the first place? We were born complete. We were born unselfconscious. As a newborn baby we expressed ourself with ease. When we were hungry we cried until we got fed. When we were happy we gurgled with pleasure. However, as soon as we were born we became conscious to those around us. We started to learn that certain behaviours, certain parts of ourself were acceptable and certain parts were unacceptable. As a result of this consciousness we started to repress parts of ourself and as we moved through the first half of life many of these got repressed deeper and deeper within our psyche.

Compared to other animals on the earth, humans are born particularly vulnerable and this vulnerability is there for a long time. This makes us very dependent on those who care for us. As a young boy you looked around yourself and saw what kind of behaviour satisfied your mother, your father and significant others in your life. You learnt that to take care of yourself you had to meet others' expectations. You evaluated what behaviour was rewarded and what behaviour was not rewarded. To live a personally successful life as a young man, you determined how you could be safe and, later, powerful rather than simply vulnerable. You also learnt to control and limit your environment so you wouldn't place yourself in situations where you felt overly vulnerable. You acted as a kind of inner parent to your inner child. This inner parent can be a fairly rejecting parent of much of your being. It is always essentially rational and so must do everything it can to keep you away from pain and hurt. Keeping away from your vulnerability was the only way you knew of dealing with your inner child.

In the 1950s and 1960s a baby's gender greatly influenced perceptions about what sort of upbringing and behaviour was acceptable. Research has shown that boys and girls are treated differently from birth onwards. The same baby dressed up in girl's clothes and then boy's clothes will be treated differently by hospital staff and visitors in the hospital nursery. A baby girl will be cooed at and handled gently while a baby boy will be treated more roughly. So even as a newborn baby boy you were treated differently to a newborn baby girl. You started to learn that certain parts of yourself were acceptable and even rewarded and some were unacceptable. Because you were vulnerable and needed those around you to care for you, you started to repress parts of yourself that didn't please these people you were dependent upon.

With the introduction of television when you were young, you could also not help but be influenced by shows such as *Superman*, *The Cisco Kid*, *The Lone Ranger* and even *Father Knows Best*. The messages from these programs only reinforced the messages sent to you by your parents, your teachers and society in general. They all emphasised the importance of power, achievement and self-control for boys. Certain messages were sent wherever you looked.

'Big boys are tough and don't cry.'

'You mustn't let anybody get the best of you.'

'Men know what to do.'

When you fell over and scraped your knee and started to cry, mum and dad quickly said, 'Be a little man, don't cry'. You learnt to stiffen your upper lip, keep your feelings under control, and get on with life. You learnt to stop crying when you felt pain. You learnt to bury your emotions deep inside yourself. Perhaps you mentioned to your dad at the evening meal that a boy was picking on you at kinder. Dad advised, 'Don't let him get the best of you. Fight back.' And so you learnt to be aggressive when you felt threatened. You learnt to fight.

Fairly quickly you realised that your fearful little boy, your insecure little boy, your vulnerable little boy, your not-knowing little boy and your scared little boy were all unacceptable. You repressed them all. As you got older you were also told that to get on you needed to work hard. Your parents had experienced the Depression and the Second World War. They passed on to you their work ethic and their attitudes about responsibility. So to meet everybody's expectations, often you learnt to repress your joyful and spontaneous nature as you channelled much of your energy into achieving. So you may add to your list of repressed selves your joyful little boy and your spontaneous little boy.

In the process of repressing all of these selves in the first half of life many of the qualities that make us human—such as compassion, trust and vulnerability—also became repressed. As a result, by the time a man reaches midlife he can feel isolated from his partner, his family, his colleagues, his friends and his own inner feeling world. It is a process we can see reflected not just in individuals, but also collectively as we watch world politics mirror this lack of balance, this lack of wholeness.

MOVING TOWARDS BALANCE

Somewhere between the age of 35 to 45 your psyche is pushing you to reclaim these repressed selves. The wonderful thing about reclaiming repressed parts of yourself is that at the same time you also become more complete in your Self, and more balanced, tolerant and open-minded in your approach to yourself, to others, and to life in general. As you do this personal work, you also reclaim more of your life force, because you are reclaiming important parts of your Self. This process of integration of your repressed selves takes many years. It goes on all your life, until you die; however, it is at its most potent at midlife.

BECOMING MORE CONSCIOUS

At midlife transition your two main developmental tasks are to find out more about your own true nature and to create a world where you can express that increasing understanding of who you are. If you are to work towards achieving the first task you have to develop a heightened level of awareness. This is not an easy task. During the first half of life you have identified with some parts but you don't even know it. You have repressed other parts in your unconscious with no knowledge that you have done so. However, there are clues that can help you on the road to increased awareness. The people and situations you have a strong dislike for, that trigger a strong emotional response in you, that you overvalue or undervalue—these are the direct projections into your outer world of your repressed, inner selves. For example, if you have spent the first half of your life showing to the world that you are a person who is strong, this will be part of your conscious understanding of yourself. It is a part of yourself that you own and are aware of.

Because the psyche always keeps itself in balance, to counteract this conscious part of yourself, buried in your unconscious is the opposite attitude, the vulnerable part of yourself. At midlife your psyche is encouraging you to claim these unconscious parts of yourself by pushing them to the surface of your awareness. As a result, at midlife you might suddenly find that you are feeling vulnerable in a situation where you haven't in the past. If you are personally aware, you will notice and acknowledge this part of yourself. You realise that as well as being strong, you are vulnerable. Over time, this aspect in your psyche becomes balanced. On the other hand, as the psyche brings your vulnerable self to surface awareness you may not acknowledge this as part of yourself. Instead, you may project this part of yourself out onto your world, often onto another person. You are rejecting of them because you perceive them as acting vulnerably. They may or may not in reality be demonstrating vulnerability. You reject their perceived vulnerable behaviour, perhaps belittle them when they display it, just as you do in relation to this attribute in yourself. Therefore a danger at midlife of not claiming repressed parts of yourself is that they can cause difficulties in your relationships with others as you overreact to people and situations around you. For you do not have control of anything that remains in your unconscious.

As you integrate many of your previously repressed selves you make them part of your conscious understanding of who you are. You can then access them at any time you choose. The emphasis here is on choice. If they remain in your unconscious they can suddenly start expressing themselves—but this will not be at your choosing and it might lead to embarrassing behaviour or lead you to unconsciously making choices that don't serve your true Self. So, another benefit of reclaiming repressed parts of yourself is that you start to live more consciously. For example, you start acknowledging and accepting both your vulnerable side and your strong side. Both become conscious to you and you are then able to use them appropriately in your world.

For some men, especially those in positions of power, a point can be reached where the split between their inner vulnerable self and their outer, high-achieving self becomes too wide. They can then develop a strong anxiety reaction. They may go on year after year suffering from this excruciating split, not even knowing much of the time that the split is there and not understanding why they are experiencing such debilitating anxiety and insecurity. And this lack of awareness of their inner world can wreak havoc as they project these unconscious parts of themselves onto their outer world.

CONNECT WITH YOUR OWN THOUGHTS, FEELINGS AND STORY AS YOU READ

There are many attributes that you will balance out in your psyche as you move through midlife transition, reclaiming repressed, unconscious parts of yourself. So far I have mentioned some of the most commonly repressed selves for men from the baby boomer era. These are the fearful, insecure, vulnerable, scared, not-knowing, joyous and spontaneous selves. Do you need to reclaim any of these at midlife? Are there other attributes not mentioned here that you may have repressed? A way of discovering the answer to these questions is to ask yourself:

- In what situations do I feel utter exhilaration?
- In what circumstances do I overreact, and later regret my actions?
- Who do I idolise, perhaps more than is really warranted?

Men at midlife experience their self-awakening in a variety of ways. How do they do this work of reclaiming repressed parts of themselves? They have few models for personal growth and change at midlife from the previous generation. From my interviews I found that when men first experience the bewildering feelings of midlife awakening they usually 'pull themselves up by their boot straps' and continue in their life, hoping these feelings will pass. They know they don't feel the way they used to but they have little idea about what to do about it. As they become aware of these feelings it is unlikely they will share them with male friends. In the first half of life men have learnt not to share their feelings with each other and, if a man does, he fears being seen as 'weak'. A man might share his feelings with his partner, although equally he might not, still fearful of showing his vulnerability. So during the early part of midlife transition a man often continues to go to work and attend to personal matters, struggling to make sense of these unfamiliar, unsettling feelings, while increasingly feeling disengaged from everything around him. This may lead to depression and illness.

The men I interviewed found a variety of ways to reclaim formerly repressed, or perhaps never-known parts of themselves. Some talked about the importance of spending time alone daily with themselves. This is often a significant step for baby boomer men as they were influenced by a society that does not encourage introspection or self-reflection. Some of my interviewees had learnt to enjoy the solitude of living alone and doing what they wanted to for the first time in their lives. Others talked about how they had learnt at midlife to demonstrate their loving self, their joyful self, their spontaneous self and their playful self through contact with their children. Some men talked about the important place of attending counselling, seminars and retreats to obtain deeper self-understanding. Others talked about the immense relief in learning to show the more vulnerable and caring parts of themselves to other men as they participated in a men's group.

For many men, an important aspect of creating a new personal world at midlife was to reclaim their spontaneous, joyful, playful and creative selves. To do this they had to get in touch with doing things because they enjoyed them and found them personally satisfying, rather than because they were good at it, or because society said they should do it or because it was a useful thing to do.

In the following chapters we will further explore midlife transition. We will listen to the voices of interviewees as they explore their thoughts and feelings about this time of midlife, and talk about how they supported themselves as they started to reclaim their repressed selves and to create a life that reflects this increased understanding of who they are. As you read *Men Navigating Midlife* I invite you to connect with your own thoughts, feelings and story. As you do, consider whether you are willing to try some of the strategies offered in order to reclaim repressed parts of yourself, to become more whole, to create a life that reflects more of the person you were born to be.

CHAPTER 4

a metaphor for understanding midlife transition

There is a river that runs through our lives, an underground stream that carries our essential being . . . Once we have entered into the stream . . . life is no longer life in the ordinary sense. Life becomes a journey, an adventure . . . Problems become teachings. Adversaries become our teachers. Illness becomes an opportunity for change and growth . . . Relationships deepen . . .

Dr Hal Stone, *Embracing Heaven and Earth*

METAPHORS HAVE BEEN USED throughout the ages to provide an enriching and meaningful framework for understanding. Our psyche speaks to us through symbols and that is why metaphors provide a powerful tool for exploration of our life experiences. I had been searching for a suitable metaphor for this book when, one morning while meditating, it came to me. It all started with a train of thought brought on by a comment a friend had made to me the day before: 'I am amazed how quietly confident you are about getting your residential courses off the ground next year.' I responded that it wasn't so much that I was confident but that I had the attitude that if I was meant to be running retreats they would work out, and if I wasn't meant to be, they probably wouldn't. I would certainly do all I could to make them happen, but after that I would just trust.

As I sat meditating, I reflected on this conversation. As I did I had a vision of myself floating down a river, the river of my life. I was in a canoe. I realised this was how I felt about my life. As long as I stay centred on myself, with an awareness of what is happening around me, I know I can mostly stay balanced in my canoe and trust my life to flow to where it should. Certainly at times my canoe and I become unbalanced or stuck as we go through turbulence or back-waters; however, I now feel I have the skills to get back on course and once again journey the river of my life. And that was when I knew I had the metaphor for this book.

As you read my metaphor I invite you to use it and the 'river of your life' map to consider where you are on your own midlife journey. Ask yourself such questions as: Am I still on the river bank? Have I found my canoe? Am I in the middle of the rapids or stuck in a side stream? Do I feel as though I am drowning? Am I connecting with my inner guide? Am I sitting mostly at ease in my canoe journeying the river of my life?

Don't worry if you can't place yourself as yet. As you continue to read the following chapters you will gradually get a sense of where you are on your own unique midlife journey.

JOURNEYING THE RIVER OF YOUR LIFE

At some time around 40 years of age you start sensing there is another way to live. Perhaps you have an inner voice telling you that this is so. Or you wake up one morning feeling depressed, realising you have no idea who you really are. Or a sudden change in your outer world—illness in yourself or another, a significant relationship ending, loss of a job—has made you start questioning all the assumptions you have been living by. Or you just realise you can't live your life the same way any longer. Whatever the reason, you now find yourself drawn to the river of your life. You walk tentatively along the edge of the river bank searching for your canoe. It is muddy and at times you wonder what you are doing there. You meet others wandering along the river bank, but mostly you are alone as you go on your search.

Finding your canoe

Eventually you find your canoe buried in the marshes. It looks strangely familiar. It also looks old and you wonder if it will hold you. You stride back to your old life and look around to see what you want to take with you. In the back of your mind you are hoping to recreate much of the good things of your old life in the new one. You head for the river loaded up with all your personal treasures. As you load up your canoe you realise you have way too much personal baggage. So even before you set out on your journey you start asking yourself, 'What is important to me now? What do I no longer need?' You make some hasty decisions about what to leave behind, pack your canoe with the rest of your belongings, and paddle out into the middle of the river.

Connecting with your story

You and your canoe feel very shaky. As you start to paddle down the river you think about your life—your long-term relationships, your career, your life in general. You and your canoe feel heavy. You have a deep sadness in the pit of your belly. To distract yourself from your feelings you keep busy moving your possessions around. Perhaps you decide at this stage that these feelings are too much to bear. If you do, you push your way back to shore, get out of your canoe, and bury it once again in the marshes. You never quite forget that it is there, but for the moment all those feelings are too difficult to encounter.

If you decide to continue your journey you experience strong feelings as you think about your life. The water around you is turbulent. It takes all your effort to not fall in and be engulfed by all the swirling currents. You feel alone. You feel pain. You feel scared. You feel sad. You feel confused. It isn't easy to explore all those memories buried long ago and to confront forbidden feelings. You paddle around a curve in the river and get caught in a snag. You are unable to move one way or the other. You feel stuck, lethargic, disillusioned and depressed as you try to find your way through. Eventually an inner knowing tells you it is best to just sit still and wait. You start to move, only to get caught in a backwater. You wonder, 'Is life just going to pass me by? Would it be easier if the canoe capsized and I drowned?' Your old life feels a long way away and you have no idea where you are going. You had no idea the journey would be so difficult. You start wondering if your old life wasn't so bad after all. Perhaps you have made a mistake. Perhaps you have been too hasty. Perhaps it's not too late to go back.

You sit as if in a trance. You don't know what you feel or think anymore. Your canoe approaches a deep, high-walled canyon. You sense its isolation. It is a gorge of tears. You have little sense of control as tears and grief pour out of you. It is as if a dam has burst inside you and there is now no holding back. All the tears have to be shed as you open your being to your own depths. As your tears start to flow you hear voices from your past saying, 'Big men don't cry. You have to be strong.'

Just when you feel it is all too much you come to a junction and meet a fellow traveller. He notices your distress, offers you support and helps you to challenge these attitudes from the past and discard them. You share your stories. It feels good to talk and share. You invite him to get into your canoe, but he reminds you that each person has their own way to navigate the river of their life. You go your separate ways.

Balancing your canoe

You yearn for aspects of your old life and from time to time you tie up your canoe and join others on the river bank. For a while the familiarity of the old ways of being are comforting as they distract you from the turbulence on the river. You race around eating, drinking and partying. Women also create a welcome diversion. For at times it feels good to distract yourself from the difficulties of navigating the river of your life. However, after a while you can't help but notice the return of tiredness, moodiness, headaches and addictions. As you reflect on your life you are drawn back to the river.

You are delighted to find your canoe where you left it camouflaged under a bush. There is relief as you get back into it. You feel tired from all the activity on the river bank. You want to lie down, but you realise there is not enough room. You need to discard more personal baggage. You ask yourself: 'What is most important to me now? What from my old life no longer serves me? What is there from my old life that will help me to journey the river of my life?'

You throw away more personal baggage. There is plenty of room to lie down now. An added bonus is that your canoe is now easier to manoeuvre and to keep balanced on the water.

You lie back and float along the river. You relax for the first time in ages. Expecting no more than a few minutes' peace, you are surprised when something unusual happens. Enveloped by the sounds of the river and the scents of the flowering gum trees on the river bank, you start to imagine how it would feel to be like the river— to flow effortlessly; to not rage against all the hazards; to not get impatient with the backwaters; to not get tense in the rapids. As you imagine this your body grows light. The sounds of the river and the buzzing insects take on a magical quality. You feel as if you are being cradled in the warmth and light of the universe. You feel at one with the world. For the first time in your life you sense you are being led towards your life purpose.

After being enveloped by this rapture you start to become fearful. Will it stay? Will it come again? As soon as these thoughts cross your mind, the magical state begins to fade. The scene is still beautiful. The flowering gum trees, the river, the rocks and the buzzing insects are all still there. However, no longer is the scene so luminous. When will you again feel such joy and oneness? You try to remember what you did before. How did you get to that state? You remember and make yourself still again while sitting in your canoe. You wait. Nothing happens. As you ponder your experience you begin to accept that you have been given a gift—a fleeting experience of wholeness. You will never forget that moment.

Your inner compass helps you navigate

As you continue down the river you have to negotiate a variety of hazards. Rocks, raging currents and rapids seem to be around many corners. You fear this turbulence and use your paddle to push away from it. Soon you realise this is futile. You let go. You sit in your canoe. You feel the turbulence and after a while you sense an inner knowing about what you need to do. You notice that when you feel fear, your canoe becomes unsteady and it is hard to keep afloat on the river. When you give in to the flow of the river, you are guided to what you need to do. You are learning to use your paddle to make your way between these hazards. Sometimes you paddle yourself to the river bank, get out of your canoe, carry it along the river bank, and then re-enter the river. It's only when you look back do you realise there was a large waterfall that could have been the end of you if you hadn't found new ways of travelling. Your inner wisdom is guiding you.

As you continue your journey you realise that the hazardous times are often a turning point as you are forced into a new way of perceiving yourself; a new way of looking at your world; a new way of navigating your life. As an unexpected current comes along and sweeps you towards unknown places you start to anticipate a new awakening. Previously you wanted to paddle away from the turbulence; now you look forward to navigating your way through to see what awaits you. As you develop the courage to do all it takes to move with and through the swirling currents, you feel more balanced in your canoe; your life takes on a new meaning; you feel more vitality in your being.

You now accept that you have an inner guiding system to show you the way through all the hazards. As you come to forks in the river

illustrated by Patricia Hay

or hazards to navigate you ask yourself questions and then listen for the answers from your inner voice. Questions such as: 'What is the right decision for me? What are my feelings telling me? What is my inner guide telling me to do? What direction do I really want for my life?'

Outer support helps you navigate

You still have times of despair; however, you have now met others on a similar journey to yours and you know you don't have to do it all by yourself. Your canoe now feels so much lighter. It takes less effort to stay balanced. A huge burden has been taken off your shoulders as you no longer feel alone. You feel calm as you sit in the middle of the river of your life. You have learnt to use your paddle to make the choices you need to make. You have an inner guiding system to help you along the way. There will still be lots of hazards, turbulence and rocky times ahead but you now have an inner sense that as long as you keep navigating the river of your life, you are living the life you were put on this earth to live.

PART 2

Finding your canoe

befriending your Self

Meditation can transform ordinary, everyday existence
and survival into something meaningful and wonderful.

Ian Gawler, *Meditation Pure and Simple*

AT MIDLIFE OUR PRIMARY developmental task is to find out more about our own true nature so we can create a second half of life that is congruent with the person we really are. But how can we do this? How do we find our canoe? When we want to befriend another person we spend time with them, ask them questions about themselves, and then carefully listen to their answers. We also spend time observing them, developing an understanding of what they like and dislike, what engages them, what moves them, what upsets them. We can use these same principles to befriend our Self at midlife and as we do, we find out about our own true nature.

At midlife we sense within us unsettled feelings such as sadness, lethargy and lack of meaning. It is important for us to find ways to acknowledge these feelings. They are there for a reason. They are asking us to look within to find out more about our own true nature. Because we are conditioned to be fearful of these uncomfortable feelings, our tendency can be to keep very busy to distract ourselves from them. This is the exact opposite of what we need to do. We need to learn to sit with ourselves, as we would with a friend and to listen to what our inner voice is wanting to communicate to us. This is very difficult for many of us to do. We will do anything else, rather than just 'be' with ourselves, especially as we start experiencing the emotionally turbulent feelings that are so common at midlife.

We can befriend our Self on four levels—physically, emotionally, intellectually and spiritually. Our physical body is like a car—when something needs attention the warning lights come on. It seems pretty obvious when stated, yet how many of us, when we have a headache, a backache, a skin rash—think the only solution is to use some medication to take these signs away? Perhaps we should also ask, 'Why is my body responding this way?' 'What do I need to attend to?' Second, we can befriend our emotional self by developing practices that help us to notice our emotions. Are we feeling contented, depressed, disengaged or lonely? Are we relating well to those around us? Many of us have had little practice in describing our feelings beyond saying we are feeling good or bad or okay. If we expand our vocabulary of descriptions for our feelings, we can increase our ability to identify our different feeling states. The 'Table of feeling words' in Chapter 10 can assist in identifying your emotions.

Third, we can befriend our intellectual self by seeking answers to such questions as, 'Am I overstimulated, bored or intellectually content by my life?' 'Am I using my intellect to create a life that suits me?' Finally, we can befriend our spiritual self by asking, 'Do I feel connected to my inner spirit and centred in my life? Do I have a sense of the meaning and purpose of my life?' Finding answers to these questions is not easy and we may never satisfactorily answer some questions in this lifetime. However, in the process we open ourselves up to finding out more about our own true nature and can then start creating a second half of life congruent with the person we are.

There are a variety of things we can do at midlife to befriend our Self, and we all need to find the strategies that best suit us. We can write in a journal our innermost thoughts and feelings. We can notice our dreams and then find ways to analyse them. We can observe ourselves as we move through our day. We can engage in deep contemplation about our life as we listen to music or gaze at the ocean when we are fishing in our favourite spot.

I am going to describe several practices I have found useful to assist the process of befriending your Self. These practices are journal writing; meditation or sitting with yourself; reflecting on and reviewing your day; and noticing your dreams. Some of the men I interviewed also found these practices useful at midlife. Others had different strategies, as they will explain later in the book.

JOURNAL WRITING—BEING YOUR OWN BEST COUNSELLOR

When I was a teenager I wrote in a journal. In this journal I wrote about what I did in my day; however, there was very little written in it about my innermost thoughts and feelings. During my teenage years my mother was dying from breast cancer, and although this traumatic event was unfolding before my eyes there was an unspoken taboo in the family about discussing what was happening to her. To manage my day-to-day life I hid many thoughts and feelings inside me. My journal was just full of events—they were safe to write about.

These days I still might write about events in my journal. Now, however, there is always an accompanying expression of innermost feelings and thoughts about these events. Whenever I have 'difficult' feelings and thoughts swilling around inside me, I find relief by picking up my journal and writing them down. I almost always find it easy to connect with my innermost thoughts and feelings, but if I ever feel stuck there are a few strategies I have found useful. For example, if I have difficulty identifying why I have strong feelings around a particular person, in my journal I will write them a letter. Just writing, 'Dear such and such', puts me into a different space internally. I feel less self-conscious and it is as though I am having a direct conversation with them. I don't send the letter. That's not the point of writing it. My aim is purely to better understand the feelings and thoughts inside me because I then understand more about my Self. Another strategy I sometimes use is to use the stem, 'I feel —— because ——' and write, not lifting my pen until I've filled a page, and see what comes out.

If you do not already have a journal I suggest you go to your local newsagent and choose a lined or unlined book, whichever appeals to you. Consider the size you want, the type of cover and so on. Then keep it in a private space, but easily accessible to you, and start writing in it. And as you find ways to express your innermost thoughts and feelings in your journal you will find that you can become your own best counsellor.

MEDITATION

The simplest and, from my interviews, the most common way a man will first befriend himself is to learn to sit with himself. It is a simple form of meditation. Until we have learnt a little about meditation we can imagine it to be a complex practice that takes years to master. This is not necessarily so. If we have the right attitude towards meditative practice—that is, not getting overanxious about getting it right, seeing it purely as a time when we sit with ourself, accepting whatever arises as we would with a good friend—we can be surprised at the outcome.

Clients often say to me that they can't find the time to meditate. This is of course one of the very reasons why meditation would be so beneficial to them. We have to be creative at midlife about how we lead our life. Some of the men I interviewed set aside a particular time each day for meditation, others just took the time when it was available. Others, such as Manny in Chapter 21, take many brief moments in their day to centre on themselves, rather than one longer meditation session. I have found this to be my own preferred practice. Whereas in the early stages of midlife transition I meditated twice a day for 20 minutes and found great benefit in doing so, these days I stop often during the day for a moment to centre on myself. At the beginning of midlife transition I needed meditation as a way of dealing with a backlog of inner work. Now my inner work is attended to through a variety of practices throughout the day. I no longer feel the need for regular, long periods of meditation twice a day, although it still can be part of my practice. You need to work out what best suits you.

If you would like to learn to meditate there are many places that will teach you for very little charge, and often no charge. For local information about courses look in the Yellow Pages®, in a wellbeing-focused newspaper, on the noticeboard of your local library or health food shop or in the Council of Adult Education course guide. Many books about meditation are available and you may decide to teach yourself, although I think it does help at first to have the support of a teacher and a group to meditate with. Below are notes on meditation. Start putting them into practice today and observe the differences in your physical, emotional, intellectual and spiritual wellbeing.

A simple meditation technique

Meditation allows us to temporarily close off from the outside world and to give time to ourself. Taking the time to bring a more relaxed, balanced feeling into our being allows us to remain more centred within ourself during our day. At first it is useful to find something on which to focus our mind as a way of shutting off from constant 'busy' thoughts around everyday concerns. This focus is just a tool to quieten our mind. Eventually we might be able to go to that still place without it. We can use this technique any time during the day when we feel the need to give time to ourself. Some people find it best to meditate in the morning, others in the late afternoon. Most people find it impossible to meditate at night; they just fall asleep.

Here are some steps you might find useful.

- *Sit in a quiet, comfortable place and close your eyes.*
- *Deeply relax all your muscles by breathing in and then as you breathe out imagine any tension in your body flowing out with your breath.*
- *Breathe through your nose in a relaxed way. Choose something to focus on. It may be where you feel the air moving in and out of your nostrils, or an affirmation such as, 'I am relaxed'. Experiment and find whatever feels best for you.*
- *It is important to not worry about whether you are relaxing. Let it happen to you at its own pace. You will get distracting thoughts. Don't fight them. Rather, acknowledge them and then let them pass on and return to your focus.*
- *Continue for as long as you have the time. It may be a couple of minutes—it may be much longer. You may open your eyes to check on the time, but do not use an alarm as it is unsettling. When going into a place of deep meditation I have found that I usually spontaneously return to my everyday awareness after about twenty minutes.*
- *When you have finished, sit quietly, at first with your eyes closed and later with them open. Do not stand up immediately as it can be jarring to the senses after being still.*
- *Practise this once, twice or many times a day, but not within two hours after eating, as digestion will interfere with your ability to relax.*

The men I interviewed noticed a variety of effects when they made meditation part of their lives. Richard felt calmer, more focused in his life and related to people better. Manny spontaneously smiled and laughed during the day and felt a sense of joy for no particular reason. Michael had insights that guided him to make significant changes in his work at midlife.

REFLECTING ON AND REVIEWING YOUR DAY

Another way of using this sitting practice is to combine it with a focus of reflecting on and reviewing your day. In the early morning you can reflect on the day ahead, centring yourself on your priorities for that day, and on how you wish to be as you go about your day. I have a personal list written on a card that I keep in my journal. On it I have written my values, the activities I want to include as part of every day, and a list of goals I want to achieve for that year. This list has come from a yearly review I carry out at the beginning of the year. For example, one of my values is 'to go about my day with a loving intent'; a daily activity is 'to physically exercise'; a focus for this year is 'to continue to develop my skills in communicating in an open and clear way when relating to others'. This reflective time early in the morning encourages me to focus on what is most important to me as I go about my day. Sometimes I am quite good at achieving my intent, other times I'm not, but with this early morning practice I am supporting myself to create the life I want. I then review the day before going to sleep at night. By looking back on what has happened during my day I develop a better understanding of my Self and the way I am relating to my world. Sometimes I might do this as I am lying in bed, just before going to sleep, other times I sit in an armchair in my bedroom.

With these practices I have gradually learnt to reflect on changes in my physical body, my emotions, my mind and my spirit as I have experienced various situations and people during my day. Whereas once upon a time I raced through my day being very busy but without noticing what had suddenly triggered an upset stomach, a feeling of unease, anxiety or a lack of centre, through reflection I now notice these reactions. I notice that when I am with certain people, or doing certain activities my 'selves' are affected. It is important to have this awareness as it helps me to make the changes I need to if I am to continue to create a world to suit the person, the Self

I am continually discovering I am. At first I had to be very conscious about this practice. Now, like any routine, it is quite automatic. Today, when I notice unsettling physical sensations and emotions I ask myself immediately, 'What has happened to make me feel this way?' There is always a powerful insight about the interplay between my Self and what is happening in my life.

NOTICING OUR DREAMS

Dreams are a powerful source for Self-understanding at midlife. They offer the most direct way to access our inner world. Like other aspects of our life we need to attend to our dreams and take them seriously if we are to make use of them on our midlife journey. Therefore, as we would with a friend, we should spend time with our dreams, not judging them quickly, but rather listening to them carefully. As we become familiar with our dreams we become familiar with the most direct way to access our inner world.

We all dream; however, some people remember their dreams much more easily than others. I don't easily remember my dreams unless I make a conscious effort to do so. Through listening to what others have to say about noticing dreams and through self-observation I have found certain understandings helpful in making best use of my dreams. Some of these understandings are:

- I am the best person to interpret my own dreams. Talking it over with somebody else might help me to understand a dream's meaning for me; however, I do not want them to give me their own interpretations.
- It is important for me to not take the dream images literally, for our psyche speaks to us through symbols. For example, if I dream about a death it does not necessarily mean that there is going to be a death in my own life. It could mean symbolically, for example, that some aspect of myself or my life is ending.
- I am more likely to focus on the symbolic nature of the dream if I consider it as an image rather than as a word description.

- It is important to focus on the feeling tone of the dream. What is my mood upon waking? What are the emotional reactions of the dreamer in the dream? What feelings do I have about the dream? What would I feel like if this situation happened to me in real life? Have I experienced similar feelings in my waking life recently that could relate to this feeling?
- If I try to understand the dream too quickly I may move on from it before I have gained all the insights I could from it. If I allow my dream to be present to me over several days, weeks or months, I usually gain many insights about the meaning of the dream.
- It helps to put into place a simple process to remember my dreams and the more I practise, the easier it becomes.

A simple process to remember dreams

- Buy a 'dream book' to draw or write your dreams in.
- Place it and a pen beside your bed.
- Say to yourself before going to sleep, 'I'd like to have a dream tonight'.
- Discuss with your partner what you are doing and ask for acceptance for you to turn on the light during the night if you need to write a dream down.
- As you wake don't open your eyes immediately but ask yourself, 'Did I have a dream last night?'

I will describe a dream of one of my clients to illustrate how effective noticing our dreams can be. During the week before visiting me he had dreamt of an unknown woman. She looked in need of care. He was baffled by the dream because her image had stayed with him since the dream. He couldn't remember whether she was young or old, although he was worried it might mean something about his ageing mother whom he hadn't contacted in several months. They did not have an easy relationship. I encouraged him to look at the dream symbolically and to understand that usually the various images in a dream represent a different part of his own psyche. I asked him: 'What part of you could the woman represent?' Over the next few weeks as he befriended his dream, he came to understand that the neglected women in his dreams symbolised the feminine, feeling part of himself that he had neglected over the years. This type of dream is not uncommon for men at midlife.

CREATING A LIFE THAT REFLECTS OUR SELF

It is vital to develop practices at midlife to befriend our Self. If we don't develop a clear idea of what is important to us, what easily angers us, what gives us a headache, what brings energy into our being, what activities help us centre on our Self, we can easily end up making decisions and ultimately creating a life that does not reflect the person we truly are. It doesn't matter if every now and again we make the wrong decision; however, if we spend our days, weeks and months making a series of wrong decisions we can end up creating a second half of life that is jarring for our being. It's like walking around with the wrong sized shirt on. It might look okay to another person but we know it doesn't fit. And this lack of fit creates stress in our life and if it continues over a long period of time can lead to:

- a poor sense of wellbeing
- difficulty in relating to others because we tend to be abrupt and short-tempered
- poor concentration leading to inability to do things as easily as we know we can
- lack of productivity
- lack of creativity and feeling 'stuck' in life
- psychological problems expressed as moodiness, depression and anxiety attacks

- feeling disconnected from life
- ill health—backache, headaches, skin conditions, immune diseases, heart problems, cancer.

As we find ways to befriend our Self we can be surprised at how fulfilling life becomes as we create a life that is just the right 'fit' for us. It doesn't necessarily mean that life is easy, for personal growth and change is not like that. However, as we develop the skills to navigate the hazardous and rocky times and backwaters, we are blessed with an increased understanding about our Self and what in the world brings us greatest satisfaction.

CHAPTER 6

depression brings its own unique wisdom

If we persist in our modern way of treating depression as an illness to be cured only mechanically and chemically, we may lose the gifts of soul that only depression can provide . . . The soul apparently needs amorous sadness. It is a form of consciousness that brings its own unique wisdom.

Thomas Moore, *Care of the Soul*

DEPRESSION CAN BE seen as a normal psychological response at midlife as we start to experience symbolically the end or death of the first half of our life and all our unrealised dreams that are contained within it. Would you recognise the symptoms of depression if you had them? What would you do if you thought you were depressed? One of my interviewees, Peter, was experiencing classical symptoms of depression but his doctor misdiagnosed his condition. He did eventually receive the correct diagnosis and assistance.

Peter: Between the ages of 35 to 45 I experienced huge problems at work and in my relationships, and loss of self-esteem. I thought that external factors accounted for a lot of what happened. The Labor Party brought in affirmative action and my promotion prospects disappeared overnight. And I thought without promotion prospects what was the point of working. Money had never meant enough to me. I was a maths lecturer at university and in the maths faculty there were 60 men and two women. Under the new legislation there was a quota that by the year 2003 there would be equal numbers, so it was obvious they would have to shed men in our faculty. This was devastating for me. I thought at first it wouldn't be taken seriously; however, when I went for a previously expected promotion I was told no. I fought the discrimination. There was an internal panel of all women and it was clear I would never get promotion.

I was furious and these feelings spilt over to women in general. Affirmative action was an absurdity. The legislation preceding it was perfectly adequate. For example, imagine if they had said half of all nurses had to be men. I was alienated from all women. I had also been fearful of the new definition of sexual assault. It was impossible to walk down aisles of students without brushing up against them. It looked to me as if the whole world was stacked up against me. My relationships with women suffered. I stopped living with the woman I had been with for ten years. I quit my job without another to go to. My whole world collapsed. I don't think that is a midlife crisis.

Robyn: Often a midlife crisis can be triggered by an outside event so it probably depends on what happened after that.

Peter: I saw a doctor. He referred me to a specialist who thought there was something physically wrong with me.

Robyn: What symptoms did you have?

Peter: I couldn't function anymore. It was all I could do to feed and clothe myself. There seemed to be no point to life. There really were severe symptoms. My memory was disturbed and my intellectual capacity was impacted. I couldn't reason properly. I had some tests that confirmed this. The strange thing is that after about a year, out of desperation, because they couldn't find any physical reason for my problem, they finally referred me to a psychiatrist.

He said that when you are depressed these are the normal symptoms and just wondered why the doctor or other specialist hadn't referred me earlier. There followed a few years of counselling which went to all sorts of factors that had nothing to do with the triggering episode.

Robyn: Can I ask what came up for you during counselling?

Peter: The most significant things went back to childhood—unresolved stuff to do with my mother abusing me. Also my tendency to fear loss and to control my environment, including the people around me, which of course was always doomed to failure. There was a repeating cycle in my relationships where in my attempt to control the person, I alienated them from me which actually doomed the relationship. The failing of the relationship made me more determined to control it and so I would go round and round in circles. An ultimate breakthrough for me was when my therapist pointed out to me that beyond haranguing a person to do exactly as I said, there was nothing I could do to control another person. I realised it was ridiculous for me to attempt to control another in the first place and as soon as I realised this, my relationships with everybody improved.

Robyn: So what made you realise this? Just by it being stated to you?

Peter: Yeah. It was stated in a very dramatic way. I can't remember how, but it was a very humorous form of counselling and suddenly I just realised it was true and that there was nothing I could do to control another. The giving up of control felt so good and this basically changed a lot of my life and the way I live it. I perhaps now have a tendency to give up too easily, because now giving up feels so good.

Robyn: So what impact did this have on you? This insight that you can't control relationships—you said it had an impact on other parts of your life as well.

Peter: It meant I could leave behind aspects of my past. For example, one of the things I had been grieving about was the loss of my academic career and work which I had found enormously fulfilling. I actually had this research that I felt really should have gone through for the good of humanity, not just for me. But then I realised that like everything else, this was an attempt to control not only how my life proceeded but also other people's lives. I realised I don't have to be that important. I knew that as a kid. I remember as a boy saying to myself there is nothing wrong with being ordinary. In fact I think it ought to be celebrated, because the alternative is to take on more than one can really expect to attain either in status or in discipline or whatever it takes to get there. So I decided to spend my time learning about all the things I hadn't yet learnt about, especially focusing on self-development. A friend told me about a series of lectures. I said I would go to one session, but she said that to give it a fair go I should contract to go to three. This worked perfectly because for the first one I had a typical reaction and I thought it was crap. By the second one I thought perhaps there is something in this, and by the third one I was totally hooked and I went to them weekly for a year and a half.

Robyn: What did you get out of them?

Peter: I learnt about a whole variety of defence mechanisms. I also found out that at a time of severe crisis our own defence mechanisms collapse. I soon realised that through the lectures I wasn't just learning about myself but also about other people. I started understanding why people are the way they are, which made it easier for me to not get so angry with them. I used to get angry a lot. I still get angry occasionally when something really obvious is not accepted by somebody else—when I think it is to their detriment. I don't know why it gets me angry—it's a vestige of the old control thing.

I also started to wonder if there was a dynamic in my life that was inevitable. I wondered if it was part of my destiny to have to give up my academic life, something I loved. In my academic life I was solving abstract problems. If anybody confronted me with a problem I had an answer for it. I now realised I had not considered all the grey areas. I started to question lots about my life, especially the question of what was the meaning of my life?

Robyn: When you think about the meaning of your life, what thoughts do you have?

Peter: Well. That's an interesting thing and I'm still not 100 per cent certain but I reckon one of them is clearly good relationships, with a lover, friends, community. In my case I don't go as far as community. I'd be happy if I had a good relationship with my lover and friends. I reckon that is hard enough. The other one for men of course is that there is an absolute driving force for sex—maybe women have that too. And then of course there are kids. I think kids will fulfil you more than anything else ever has, and you learn more through watching kids grow up than any other way. I don't have any children of my own although I love spending time with them. This can be difficult for a man on his own. For example, when I swim in our local pool I can't even say hi to the kids without their mothers looking suspiciously at me. Luckily, at the time I was having counselling I took in some boarders and two of them were a mother and her baby. Because I wasn't working I was able to help look after the baby. We have continued a close relationship and times with her are very important in my life. I love nurturing her. At midlife, times with her help me reflect back on influences in my own childhood and teenage years.

Robyn: What sort of times?

Peter: For example, recently I have been remembering my first work experience at fourteen in a storeroom at a coal mine. People in the stores were too old to do men's work such as digging up coal, or they had been injured so badly they were no longer able to do proper work. It was considered okay work for a schoolkid though. The men working with me were like the walking dead. They had no life at work and they appeared to have very little life outside work. They were dying from their own environment. Their skin was like sandpaper and a black-brown colour from the coal dust.

Back then that experience started me thinking about what I was going to do as a career when I grew up and how I was going to bring pleasure into my life. I realise I am asking of myself similar questions again, but now I am a different person.

Robyn: In what ways are you different?

Peter: In my earlier years I felt superhuman, I felt invincible. I felt I could do anything I wanted to. However, I wasn't good socially and so I was always scared about losing my girlfriend. I wondered how I would manage without her. I also hated the thought of having to look for another. It filled me with fear. These days socially I'm far more comfortable. I'm a lot more tolerant of myself and of others. I understand people's motivations these days and that makes it easier to accept differences between people. Recently I have also felt my age a lot. Until my mid-forties I felt like an eighteen-year-old. In my late forties I have aged quite dramatically. When I was eighteen and shaving I accidentally caught my eye in the mirror and I thought, 'Who's that? I don't know him.'

Robyn: How do you feel now?

Peter: (Gets up and looks at himself in the mirror) Yes, I do know him.

Robyn: In your earlier years you were a stranger to yourself but not now?

Peter: It's rather odd because you'd think if you don't know yourself you wouldn't be happy—but I was happy back then.

Robyn: But getting to know ourself fully can bring a lot of heartache because it's not just our good side we get to know. At midlife we get to know our shadow side including our limitations.

Peter: You're right. I said I was invincible. It was never a reality.

Robyn: And what about your world. How has that changed?

Peter: I stopped living for my work. The psychology of that was a bit strange. To myself I'd explained it as a deliberate act of choice roughly along the lines, 'I have no children, therefore there really is no commitment I have to live up to and so why the bloody hell am I working full time?' I suddenly realised I don't need money. I don't need it for the definition of myself. If I defined myself that way I was at the mercy of my employer and the social milieu. But I don't know the real reason for the change. I never know what other factors are there. These days I am a bit distrustful of consciously made decisions—they are often excuses for decisions you wanted to make anyway.

Robyn: So, if work doesn't define your world, what does?

Peter: The few relationships I continue—they ground me in a small community which most of the time is enough for me. Sometimes it isn't enough. Part of that is the lack of intense interaction I would like through an intimate relationship. I would like to have one person in my life where I can pull no punches and we can aim for an understanding of each other. Friendships can't give me this. Women have an advantage in that they form easier social networks. It's not just good for social support. They also have a ready-made sounding board for self-understanding. I've found relationships between men relatively superficial. I think it is a fear of showing the non-masculine side. The quickest way to lose status in a circle of men is to show weakness.

Robyn: Would it have made a big difference to you at midlife if you had been able to talk to the men around you?

Peter: Yes, it could have avoided the depth of difficulty I got into. You can't even say to a male you're not feeling okay, they'll fob you off.

Robyn: Have you tried to?

Peter: I don't know when I gave up trying. It was a long time ago. You can get a bit across through humour, but why should you?

Robyn: Have you ever thought of going to a men's group?

Peter: Yes, I have thought of it because it was one of the things recommended at the course I did. There they had groups where men and women were together, which I thought was better. It was something I avoided at the time because I thought to myself, 'Why should I need to use a group when I have friends?' I don't feel the same need these days. Now I am very satisfied with my own company. I paint. I write. I play music. When I was young there was no way I could live alone. I'd go crazy. This was probably the function of having a woman in my life.

Robyn: And now?

Peter: This need has disappeared. In fact I am probably my own best company. The arguments I hold with myself never get bitter.

MOVING THROUGH DEPRESSION

In our society there is a tendency to pathologise depression. It is often portrayed as a physical illness needing medical attention. This might be the case if there is a genetic or physiological problem. However, at a time of loss and change, it is important to recognise that it is also a normal response as we grieve our loss.

At midlife, as we start to let go of the old way of perceiving ourself and of living our life, we need to grieve. This grieving then allows us to move towards a new way of being. To support ourself at midlife we need to find ways to connect with and express our feelings. Antidepressants may assist if we are experiencing depression and if we are stuck in the grieving process, although where there is depression as part of the grieving process often the most effective support is to find a way to express our feelings. So if you are taking antidepressants, I suggest you consider concurrent counselling which allows you to express your feelings and to have them acknowledged. When depressed we can also support ourself by expressing our emotions through such activities as writing, drawing, painting and creative dance. Any form of creativity is a place of Self-expression and just doing it will lead you to a place of emotional release.

Among the men I interviewed, as with Peter, the most common method of support was to find an effective therapist, such as a psychiatrist, psychologist or qualified counsellor. If you are experiencing depression you could look in your local telephone book for a men's health help line. Or you could consult your local doctor for a suitable referral. Would you consider seeking out this sort of help if you thought you were depressed?

CHAPTER 7

illness—a call for change

*. . . if people don't express their grief, they end up
radiating grief. They get depressed. If people can't say
what they want and repress their real wants and desires,
something like cancer may overtake them.
To heal the illness, we have to heal
the underlying problem in our subconscious.*

Professor George Jelinek, *Taking Control of Multiple Sclerosis*

AT OUR FIRST MEETING Erik impressed me as a well-built,
attractive, warm man in his late forties. Ten months later we reconnected at a music festival. As we caught up on each other's news
I learnt that six months previously he had been operated on for
testicular cancer.

As Erik seemed quite comfortable talking about it I asked him
if I could interview him for this book. The next afternoon I sat
outside my tent, beside the creek, among the gum trees, listening
to his story. Later that evening, as we sat listening to music and
chatting, Erik shared further information, making his story even
more intriguing.

Erik

I was born in the Netherlands. My family was strict Presbyterian with my father the 'head' of the family. From the age of five my parents told me:

'Don't kiss us goodnight anymore. You are a big boy now.'

'You should know what to do.'

'What a good boy you are.'

When I was ten years old my father died from cancer. It was only in my forties I realised how close I was to my father. It was as though I had forgotten about him. My mother cried for two years after his death. It shattered me to see her grieve and not be able to help. However, looking back now I realise I liked my mother more afterwards. She changed. She became more tolerant. I still find it hard to be around people who are emotional. After my father's death my brother became head of the family and life was even stricter. I was always trying to do the right thing and not make mistakes, and I tried to get affection by being good.

At school I was a loner. I was good and clever and always being teased. When teased I couldn't fight back. I would just smile and bury my painful feelings, even when the boys called me dreadful names. From an early age I escaped from this loneliness by dreaming about girls. Right through my teens and early twenties I had many girlfriends but I was incredibly afraid of sex. My strict religious upbringing had told me sex before marriage was wrong. This left me totally confused. I felt as if I was in no-man's-land. I wanted to free myself but it was as though it was 'hard-wired' into me. I wanted to have experiences but was worried that if I was free with a girl she would see me as morally unworthy.

At seventeen I went to the US as an exchange student for a year and had a marvellous time. They treated me differently. People thought I was funny and clever. So from then on, as an outlet, in between my studies back in the Netherlands I travelled all over the world. I finally accepted a scholarship to Australia. It was a way of running away from the confusion of home. In Australia I met my wife, Joanna. She wasn't judgmental. She was easy and she was fun. We married and had two children. Looking back I can now see that I always lived by trying to anticipate what others wanted of me. I was always saying to myself: 'I am the only one who can sort things out.'

In our late thirties Joanna and I realised we were estranged. She started to explore aspects of herself, rediscovered her sexuality, and I felt I got dragged into something I wasn't ready for. The more she looked to herself, the more it looked like an attack on me. So we went through a really hard time. Not big arguments, but silent times. I felt despair and resentment about what I thought she was rejecting in me. She wanted me to examine myself, my fears around sexuality, and my feelings in general. But for me it translated into performance anxiety around making love. For a long time it didn't get resolved and in the meantime Joanna made her own progress by continuing her self-exploration and gaining a degree in psychology.

Four years ago I went to a three-week leadership development course through my work. The essence of the course was to take people away and for the focus to be on self-development, including others giving you feedback. I was surprised by some of the feedback including their perception of me wanting to control things. Soon after I got home Joanna and I did a tantric workshop and it helped as I could see that other people were also struggling and I felt I could talk out in the open for the first time about my problems around sex. Since then I have attended a variety of workshops and festivals. At first I was always worried about whether I would fit in, but from the first one I could see it was all in me. If I just made myself feel okay, everything was fine. Stepping out of my comfort zone made me challenge a variety of beliefs I had about myself and my world. For example, I challenged my need for approval. I realised that I was more disapproving of myself than anybody else. I had internalised my parents' disapproval more than anyone else.

Joanna then had an affair and this confirmed all my prejudices about being unworthy, not being attractive and not being accomplished enough sexually. For me it was a breaking point in our marriage. We went to a one-week tantric workshop. It was wonderful and confronting. I felt as though I did an enormous amount of development. I remember one exercise where we had to write our obituary. This really shook me up.

We came back and went to a counsellor and what came out really strongly was that we each felt the other wasn't meeting our needs. We were so busy thinking about our own needs we were not thinking about the other's. I then got work in Sydney three days a week and this seemed a good way of breaking the co-dependency. Ironically, three weeks later I discovered a lump in my testicles and I knew straight away what it was. I rang Joanna and just cried. In less than a week I was having surgery for testicular cancer, and a week after that I started chemotherapy.

The crux of the story for me is that when I was at primary school I was given the nickname 'scrotum'. It was a cruel nickname. In a prudish society it is a dirty word. I couldn't tell my parents. I just used to grin and pretend it didn't hurt me. They could always put me in place by using it. These same boys also had a cruel game where they kneed you in the groin—I felt ongoing humiliation and fear. I've always wondered if my moral upbringing made me think sex was dirty, or whether it was because of being hounded with my nickname in front of the girls at school. I always had an inner voice commenting on every action. When I got the cancer it seemed like destiny. I could now see what this was all leading up to. Inside I was saying to myself, 'Who wants sex if it creates all these problems? So chop it all off, why bother.'

I have a strange feeling of destiny or that I invoked it. I know I haven't completed the journey of who I am sexually. I can now see it is not an issue of performance but rather an issue of how I feel.

Perhaps I needed surgery before I could accept that message. It is now six months since this started and it is the first time I have had time to focus on myself. No longer am I rushing around helping others, or doing the busy things, or being a superhero. Now I lie around and feel bad. I want to learn to take it easy. I am going to counselling and that is helping. Some of the things I am learning to do are:

- I put boundaries around my rescuing behaviour. I now ask permission.
- I ask myself why I am doing things. Often, I then stop doing them. My workload is now easier.
- I've finished a change management qualification and want to start doing some consultancy work.
- I am learning to nurture myself. I went back to the Netherlands by myself and visited my brother and sisters. I asked them about their childhood. That was a real eye-opener. I was surprised. It affected each of us in a different way.
- I am doing a meditation and chanting course at a local ashram. I also practise by myself at home.
- Joanna and I have also joined a talking circle. We have a stick and when it is your turn you hold the stick and talk for up to ten minutes. Nobody can interrupt you and it is wonderful to know you have that space to talk. When you have finished everybody focuses on you and sends you healing.

My counsellor says she sees many men, especially those born since the late 1940s and 1950s, who seem to walk around with feelings of their own unworthiness. I feel that mine have resulted in the cancer.

   I can't totally picture what will happen next. Joanna and I still don't have a robust sexual relationship—because of the treatment it has been put on hold. The next year is going to be an enormous challenge. Looking back, I now wish there were some shortcuts. People ask, 'How do you feel?' I don't really feel that bad. In this last half year I've given more time to myself than I've ever done. At home I'm more open with the children. When I flew back from Sydney I hadn't thought about whether Joanna might have told the children. She had. I wondered if I would have been so open. I don't think I would have. To watch their emotional faces, and also the way they were so caring, it made me feel special. I then sent an email around to tell my colleagues about the cancer.

THE UNCONSCIOUS KNOWS

As we were sitting listening to music that evening Erik told me about a drawing he had done at the leadership course a couple of years before learning he had cancer. He had been asked to do an outline of his whole body and then to write some words and do some markings on his drawing. Over his testicles Erik had drawn a large, red cross.

In his book, *The Secret World of Drawings*, Gregg Furth explains: 'Unconscious psychic contents are conveyed in drawings, not only by the seriously ill, but also by the healthy, those whom we call "normal" individuals, both psychologically and physically. If this unconscious material is deciphered it provides highly therapeutic insight.' Furth is suggesting the power of drawing to make contact with and heal aspects of our inner, unconscious world. So, as with the interpretation of our dreams, we can receive important messages from our unconscious through our drawings. Do you think it is possible that through his drawing, Erik's unconscious was trying to give him a message about the physical problems developing as an expression of his unresolved psychological issues? If you had an illness would you just see it as a physical problem needing physical attention, or would you consider that it might be your body sending you a message from your unconscious—a message that is vital to your ongoing wellbeing?

CHAPTER 8

illusions collapsing

*Despair is the shattering of our manly illusion
of being in control that comes with the
awareness that our stance as conquerors
of life is an illusion and that we are
not 'masters of our fate' and
'captains of our soul'.*

Sam Keen, *Fire in the Belly*

THE PROCESS OF MIDLIFE transition is often triggered when one of our acquired beliefs is challenged and then overthrown. This can bring on what is commonly referred to as a 'midlife crisis'. Beliefs such as, 'If I work hard for my family I will be rewarded with a united family' or, 'When I reach my dream job I will finally be happy', can be challenged at midlife. These beliefs may not be explicitly articulated, but can be strongly held even though never discussed or acknowledged.

Were such a fundamental belief to be challenged at another time of life it would not have the same impact as it does at midlife. For at midlife our psyche is encouraging us to question all aspects of how we perceive ourself and our life—and so once one belief is found not to be true, our psyche encourages us to question them all.

OUR ACQUIRED BELIEFS ARE
INTERCONNECTED

When I was young my family often sat at our dining room table and played a game—well it was more just a fun way to pass the time—where we built houses out of playing cards. First we would lean two cards in to each other diagonally, which would form the base of the house. Then we would surround this house structure with four more cards. They created the walls of the house. Then we would create the roof by placing two cards horizontally on the top of the structure. The next challenge was to build another house structure on top of the first. At times we had a tower of up to eight houses, one on top of the other. Sometimes the house structure spread out as well as up—we started with several houses at the base and then built on all of these at the same time.

As we grow up we build a core of beliefs in a manner similar to the way I built these card houses. These beliefs help us to make sense of our world and to find a way to fit into it. And as with my card houses, all our core beliefs are interconnected, and can influence every other belief.

OUR ACQUIRED BELIEFS CREATE
OUR ILLUSIONS

In the first half of life we acquire our beliefs from those around us. First we are influenced by our parents' and teachers' beliefs, and then later by the beliefs of our peers, partners, colleagues and friends. All these acquired beliefs hang together and create a filter that affects how we perceive ourself, our life and our world. The only way we can make sense of what we see is by judging it through these current beliefs, so our mind persuades us that our perception is real. Our beliefs don't show us what reality is. All they show us is our own internal ways of representing what we have been conditioned to believe reality is. We understand something new by comparing it to something we already know. When we come across something which is actually so new to us that there is nothing in our belief system like it, we tend to quickly discount or ignore it.

Given the beliefs encouraged in a boy growing up in the 1950s and 1960s, a man might typically arrive at midlife today saying to himself: 'My partner and I have created a life together. Nothing can come between us', 'I have worked loyally. My job is secure' or, 'I am a good person. Nothing bad can happen to me.' Then one day his partner leaves him, he loses his job, or he is struck down by a life-threatening illness. He discovers one of his core beliefs is faulty. This experience can be shattering to a person's whole belief structure, especially at midlife.

Let me explain further. I will describe how a man might develop the belief, 'I have worked loyally. My job is secure', and then how he will be affected when this belief is challenged at midlife.

When young he learnt that if he did his work at school he was rewarded with a smile from his teacher. Later he was rewarded for consistent work with good grades and praise from his parents. By adulthood he holds the core belief, 'If I work hard I will be rewarded'. Then, one Monday morning, after many years of loyal work for a company, he arrives at his job and is told he is no longer wanted. His job has been made redundant. He has been made redundant. One of his acquired, core beliefs, one of his illusions, is shattered. He is shattered. When something like this happens it can feel as if you and your world are falling apart.

AT MIDLIFE OUR PSYCHE WANTS US TO QUESTION ALL OUR ACQUIRED BELIEFS

If this sort of experience happens to us in the first half of life we might just pick ourself up from this blow, shake ourself down and go and find another job. However, if we are at midlife our psyche will encourage us to question all our acquired beliefs. And as we examine our whole belief structure, much of it comes tumbling down. Just as my card houses so often did.

This experience is devastating. If it happens to you, you can feel as if you are falling apart. You aren't. Your belief structure is. This understanding can be reassuring when confronting such a crisis. If you understand that you are going through the process of dismantling your acquired belief structure so you can slowly replace it with a belief structure more closely reflecting who you truly are, it can help make sense of the experience. And this is what you need to do as you move through midlife transition. This new belief structure enables you to create a second half of life that is personally fulfilling as it is based on your own beliefs. You replan your future, perhaps build a life without your partner or the job you had such expectations of, or explore new philosophical beliefs about life. This dismantling and rebuilding can be unpleasant and scary, especially at first; however, if you understand the importance of restructuring your core beliefs at midlife you'll feel reassured as you go through it.

CHANGING YOUR CORE BELIEFS CAN BE DIFFICULT

Whether change is foisted upon you, or whether it is self-directed, choosing to change your beliefs at midlife can be very difficult. First, your relationships with others will be affected. For example, if you have always been one to want to please those around you, and then finally decide to speak and live by your own truth, family and friends won't like it. If you change, they have to change. Sure, they want you to be happy but not if it makes life less comfortable for them. So you may need to find ways to protect yourself from their influence during this time of questioning. Second, you have developed your beliefs in the first half of life because you are getting something out of them. For example, you might need to ask yourself, 'Why is it so important to me to earn a top salary?' For it is the fear of losing these sorts of benefits which can stop you from examining your core beliefs. Finally, at midlife, as you re-examine your beliefs and change how you perceive yourself and your life, you have to be willing to experience the difficult feelings of loss.

FEELINGS OF LOSS ARE NORMAL AS CORE BELIEFS COLLAPSE AT MIDLIFE

As we discard old, rigid beliefs it is normal to experience feelings that are part of the grief process. If we don't understand what feelings are normal at a time of loss and change, we can become terribly frightened as we experience such feelings as anger, despair and depression. These feelings are there to help us to let go and then rebuild, but if we get caught up in the fear of the experience we may get stuck and never make the necessary changes to create a personally satisfying second half of life.

We might resort to desperate defences so as not to experience these frightening feelings. We might get frantically busy, hoping that by being very active and pretending that everything is all right we can ignore the terror inside us. We might even think that we are going crazy as we experience anxiety and depression. Other people who share our lack of understanding may also think that we have a mental illness and describe us as manic, depressed or as having a nervous breakdown. Or they might see it as a hormonal problem. Yet all that has happened is that our belief structure has collapsed and as a result we are experiencing feelings of grief and loss.

In her classic book, *On Death and Dying*, Dr Elizabeth Kubler-Ross was the first person to clearly articulate the stages of grief and the emotions experienced when a loved one dies. It is now widely recognised that these stages and emotions equally apply when we experience any change, for in any change we experience a mini-death. The first stage of grief is disbelief and denial. For example, after a man's wife has left him he may say to himself: 'This isn't happening to me. She doesn't really mean it. Life will soon go back to normal. She'll realise she can't do without me.' Such feelings and thoughts can give a man time to get used to the change, but eventually he does need to move on to the next stage: bargaining. This stage is an attempt to deny the irreversibility of the situation. Sudden loss of a job or partner might initiate such reactions as, 'I can change', 'I can work harder', 'We should wait until the children are older' or, 'We should go to counselling'. Sometimes others will go along with the bargaining for a while. This allows time for rethinking and imagining new possibilities. Next, when we realise that the change is inevitable and that there isn't a lot we can do to go back to the old life, we experience intense feelings of anger: 'Why are you doing this when we have spent so many years building a life together?' or, 'Why am I being treated so shabbily after years of loyal service?' During this stage we may react erratically and experience fury and anger. It is important to find appropriate ways to express these emotions as they allow us to move on to the next stage.

Despair and depression now overwhelm us. We feel totally helpless. It is as if we fall into a hole. We now start questioning every belief we have lived by. This is a time when sleeping and eating patterns can be deeply affected. We don't want contact with others, yet supportive friends can make a huge difference. Professional help may be needed. If we give ourselves time, accept that these feelings are normal at a time of loss, and give ourselves the space to grieve, we support ourselves enormously. It is important not to make any significant decisions during this time as we may be eager to fill the void and a hasty choice may prove unwise.

After days, weeks, months or perhaps even years of being mainly in our own world, feelings of self-pity give way to acceptance. For some of us it is a gradual grieving and moving forward. For others it is as though one day we wake up and look at the world with new eyes. We can see a way forward. Our world is different. We are different. We can now let go enough to start moving on. Either way, we start to rebuild an understanding of who we are and what we want in our life based on a more accurate understanding of ourselves and our world.

With this understanding about what feelings are normal at a time of change and loss we assist ourselves while in the midst of turmoil by telling ourselves, 'I'm changing. My life is changing. These feelings are normal at midlife. I'll survive. By allowing myself to experience these feelings, rather than running away from them, I will eventually create a life that suits me well.' Alternatively we may cling on in fear to old beliefs such as, 'I have to have a partner to be happy' or, 'The only job that will satisfy me is one with a high income'. We hold on to our old beliefs in fear, and in the process we deny ourself the chance to find new ways of creating happiness and personal fulfilment for the second half of our life.

COMMON SOCIETAL BELIEFS OR ILLUSIONS MEN CHALLENGE AT MIDLIFE

The beliefs we have acquired in the first half of life can blind us to possibilities for the second half of our life. While focused on something that isn't even true, we can deny ourself the opportunity to open up to possibilities that bring us more personal satisfaction. Because of the way a baby boomer man was encouraged to define himself as he was moving into adulthood, many of the core beliefs that need to be challenged will be around his work, his role in the family as 'breadwinner' and his perception of himself as omnipotent.

I have listed below some common societal beliefs held by men. As you read the list, ask yourself if any of them are held by you. If so, you could then consider challenging them as it might open up new possibilities for your life.

- If I push hard enough I can do anything.
- When I have enough money I will be happy.
- If I keep control of my life I can stop problems happening.
- The harder I work the more secure I will feel.
- If only I had enough money I would not have problems.

- If I am a good provider my family will be happy.
- I'm happy in my work.
- People value me at work, I get paid well, and I am providing for my family. I should be happy.
- The more money I earn, the more successful I am.
- If I show my vulnerability I am weak.
- I have to keep on providing for my family at the level that I am—without it my whole family will collapse.
- If I only had a job I really liked I'd be happy.
- I am my work.
- If I show my emotions I have failed.
- If I seek help it means I am weak.
- If everything appears fine, it is.
- If I just think hard enough a solution can always be found.
- I am invincible. I can take my health for granted.

How many of these societal beliefs or illusions limit the way you live your life right now? Are there others that come to mind? Challenging them is not easy. As you let go of the limited ways you have perceived yourself and your world you have to move through your fears and learn to trust that as you do, you will be okay. As you choose to do this work at midlife you find creative ways to live the second half of your life. No longer are you fenced in by societal beliefs. No longer are you fenced in by your illusions!

CHAPTER 9

as fear gives way to trust

The need is not to remove fear from the world, but instead to develop in ourselves the psychic capacity to confront its destructive power. In this realm, consciousness, coupled with love, is everything. Enlarging consciousness to include an awareness of soul allows a healthy struggle with fear, and love makes possible its transformation, not just within ourselves but also within the world.

Robert Sardello, *Freeing the Soul From Fear*

I WENT OUT WITH Alf last night. I'm on holiday—well a sort of working holiday—in Byron Bay. I've been here annually for the past fifteen years and this year I've decided to have a month here, including going to the Writers' Festival as a keen onlooker.

I knew Alf in Melbourne. Not well. I joined a group last year that he had played music with for the past eight years. I was invited to come along one evening and after a while I was invited along regularly and now comprise the percussion section. Given that my djembe playing skills are still in their infancy, and that it has been a dream of mine to be involved in such a group, I jumped at the opportunity.

I remember sitting with Alf last November after one of our music group's sessions. He told me that he had decided to go to live near Byron Bay to study music. He said he had wanted to do it for five years but kept on finding reasons to put it off. I sensed he was both excited and apprehensive. Over the next couple of months I sensed that he was feeling increasingly apprehensive about the move; however, because I did not know him well I picked this up more by observation than direct conversation.

As Alf and I sat eating a delicious Indian meal in a restaurant in Byron Bay listening to the music of 'The Love Handles' he told me how happy he was. He is 51. He's now been in Byron Bay for six months. He talked about his course, his piano teacher, where he lives and of the ease of creating a life that feels just perfect for him.

Later Alf told me about the panic attacks and palpitations he had before leaving Melbourne. He said that what got him moving after five years of procrastination was when one of his friends had become really angry with him when once again he was talking about his dream, but doing nothing to make it happen. Her anger galvanised him into at last making the move, but as the time got closer his anxiety became extreme. He described the day when he finally got in his car to drive to Byron Bay. He immediately started to relax, and since that time six months ago he says he hasn't looked back. He described a series of 'little miracles' that happened from that time on to make it easy for him. And now he can't imagine doing anything else or living anywhere else.

At midlife we have a choice. We can either live within the limitations of our fears, or we can challenge them, and in the process open ourself and our life up to a much fuller reality. Many of our fears are connected to experiences from our past, especially our childhood. It is only by putting in the time to explore our unconscious and connect with these fears from our past that we are able to move on to a creative way of living and being at midlife.

Around about 35 to 40 years of age life presents us with opportunities to broaden our life experiences. In the first half of life it is normal to use our natural abilities to create a secure life structure. In the second half of life, for normal growth, and for greater balance in our being, we need to develop our neglected side. Ironically, the development of our natural abilities has allowed us to avoid areas where we don't want to go. For example, we may have learnt to be self-reliant. This can be viewed as a positive thing; however, if it has been developed at the expense of learning to rely on others, our self-reliance may have covered up a fear of trusting others. Midlife is about moving towards wholeness. To do this we need to own our natural abilities and preferences, while at the same time see our fears around the neglected aspects of our Self as the doorway to a more complete us.

As we move through midlife transition and work on our less developed side, we increasingly come to a place of balance. This balance helps us to manage all the stresses and strains of working through our fears. Certainly it's not easy. It can be a very painful, difficult place to go to. However, the reward is a more expansive understanding of ourself and a more expanded life with all the learnings, great times and difficult times that go with it. And of course if we don't open the door to look our fears squarely in the face they tend to keep on knocking at the door anyway, often making our lives increasingly restricted and uncomfortable.

TRUST VERSUS FEAR

In our culture there is a strong belief that we should run away from our uncomfortable feelings. Sometimes we are so fearful of fear that we lose our ability to make use of this valuable guide to open up to more of our being at midlife. Fear is a part of everyday life and like all our feelings, if noticed and worked through, becomes a valuable guide as we navigate 'the river of our life'. A difficulty for many men is that they have spent so many years denying their feeling world, they have no conscious awareness of fear in themselves. It is there and it is controlling their day-to-day actions, but this is all at an unconscious level. Sometimes a man may only become aware of a fear when it goes and he senses a burden has lifted.

To help be aware of fear as it arises in us, it can be useful to look at the differences between a trusting person and a fearful person. These two types of people are at either ends of a feeling state. Rarely is an individual totally in a fearful state or a trusting state. We all tend to move along a continuum between the two, depending on our responses to events in our life. Some of us will have a tendency to be more up one end of the continuum. As you read the differences between the trusting man and the fearful man, consider where you are on this continuum for much of your present life.

The fearful man is shut down to different possibilities in life and his vision for himself at midlife is narrow. He makes little attempt to look inward and any change that occurs in his life is on the outside. He might change jobs, partners or where he lives, but basically the way he approaches the second half of life remains similar to how he approached the first half of life. He is very controlling in how he lives his life, as many fears arise each time he steps out of a tightly controlled comfort zone. When he feels fear he runs away from it, rather than looking within for what it might mean. He often feels disillusioned and at midlife has stopped dreaming about new possibilities. Life for him is just doing more of the same. He continues to strive in the outer, material world and then wonders why he still has a nagging fear inside him, despite having ever more material riches.

In contrast, the trusting man understands that the most important journey to take at midlife is within himself. He realises that many of the attitudes he acquired as a child are limitations. He trusts in the process of his life, with all its ups and downs. Much of this trust comes from the strength of knowing himself well and having access to a variety of self-empowering skills that help him to trust in managing his life, no matter what arises. He continually notices his responses as he moves through his day and regularly sets aside time to look at what is coming up for him in his life. For example, if he senses fear arising in himself as he starts a new relationship or a new job, he will first consider if there is anything in his environment to warrant this response. If not, he looks within to determine what attitudes he needs to challenge if he is to respond in a more trusting, rather than fearful way. In these times of self-reflection he often reviews aspects of his childhood and gradually realises that fears taken on as a child are no longer necessary. As he does this work he feels increasingly self-empowered.

Conversely, the fearful man easily relates to the wounds of child-hood and uses them to explain his unhappiness and inability to create the life he wants. He uses his childhood experiences as an excuse rather than as a place to revisit and to move on from. He imagines that those around him who do seem to be getting on with their lives, creating new opportunities for personal fulfilment, were blessed with a childhood or a support he missed out on. He is always making excuses, procrastinating, making do, rather than believing it is possible to achieve his dreams. In fact the fearful man doesn't even try to dream anymore. His fears control him. He is not self-empowered.

FEARS ARE USUALLY EMBEDDED IN CHILDHOOD EXPERIENCE

When we feel fearful in the present it is often because memories of a situation from our past are triggered. When young we feared we would be abandoned if we didn't behave the way significant others, especially our parents, wanted us to be.

As we conformed to our world, and repressed parts of ourselves, accompanying fears were buried in the unconscious at the same time. As we move through midlife transition and want to reclaim these parts of ourself so as to become more whole, we need to become aware of the fears that made us experience this repression in the first place. As we do this work we learn to trust that no longer can we be abandoned. The only person who can abandon us now is ourself. Perhaps an example will be useful here.

We were born loving. However, if our love was rejected when we gave it to a significant other, such as a parent, we might easily become fearful of loving and lose our ability to trust in love. Now when we have difficulty showing our love to another, or of accepting love from another, we need to be able to see that the situation is different, and that we can learn to trust in love again. Certainly we need to be discerning. Perhaps there is a reason to fear entrusting our love in a certain person in the present. We can rationally assess the situation. If we see that the object of our love is consistent, kind and thoughtful in relation to us perhaps this is a place of learning. And even if at times we feel unloved in this relationship, we can see that it is different from when we were young.

We are now adult and even if things go wrong we can reassure ourself that we can look after ourself. So at midlife we learn to open ourself up to love when we make conscious these previous unconscious fears. As an adult we can then make conscious choices. We can look at the person and the situation, do the work to become aware of our unconscious fears and learn to trust in love. And each time we go through this process we learn to be more trusting of ourself, and as a result we feel more at ease within ourself and with others. This helps us to become more trusting and loving in all our relationships.

Facing our fears

In his book, *Freeing The Soul From Fear*, Robert Sardello describes what happens to our body when we become fearful:

> As fear affects us, we not only become filled with anxiety, but also find ourselves more uncomfortable in our body—it begins to feel more like an object we have to lug around. We may feel tired for no reason, filled with an ongoing sense of exhaustion. A dim but pervading sense of depression accompanies us all the time.

I find this description of Sardello's incredibly accurate for the way I experience fear. In the past I have often felt this way without having a clue about what it meant. Now I can notice how one minute I am feeling at ease in my body, a lightness in my spirit and joy for my world and then in a moment it has all changed. Without my consciously noticing, something in my outer world has triggered a response inside me, or a thought has entered my mind, and my body has gone to a place of fear. Other physical symptoms I am likely to experience are a tight, 'sicky' feeling in my gut, tightness in my shoulders or backache.

If we become aware of being fearful, what can we do? First of all we can congratulate ourself for noticing—this is certainly a step in the right direction, and not an easy one. Second, we can start trying to understand where the feeling is coming from. Yes, we are feeling fearful, but what about? At this step it is very easy for me to start looking to my outer environment to find the culprit. For example, I might start questioning the motives of somebody in my personal world. There might be a genuine reason in my outer environment for my fear. However, it is equally possible that a present situation has triggered an old fear—a fear from childhood that protected me then —but is no longer necessary. Now the fear is limiting my experience of myself and my life and if I allow my fear to control me at midlife it will restrict my ability to create a vital second half of life.

Once I have recognised there is fear inside me, and that there is nothing in my immediate outer world to warrant it, I will then use a variety of tools to try to better understand the fear within me.

PROTECT YOUR SOUL FROM MORE FEAR

First, I might decide to go about my daily activities, and include some experiences that open and relax my being. By doing this I encourage my mind to be in a relaxed state, rather than agitating on my fear. I will do some physical activity that stretches and relaxes my body such as yoga, dance or walking through nature. I will find activities to relax my mind—listening to music, lying in the sun and daydreaming or watching nature. At first, some of these activities will require effort as my body is feeling so burdened and heavy with fear. I just feel like sitting in a fearful, depressed heap. Yet once I make the effort I am rewarded by some release of emotion and insight about my inner state as my body relaxes.

If I overload my body with more fears my senses 'dumb down' even more and I am less likely to gain insight into my fear. So at these times of fear I protect myself from bringing more fear into my being. There are several practices I observe at these times of fear and even follow day to day as a way of 'freeing my soul from fear'. Because men have been taught to tough out their fears some of these ideas may challenge you; however, I suggest you try them next time you feel fearful and then reflect on how useful they are.

- I ensure I don't read material that will increase the feeling of fear within my mind. For example, I may choose to only read select parts of the newspaper, if at all.
- I won't watch anything on television that is likely to raise the feeling of fear inside me. I certainly don't watch any horror movies.
- I am careful about what types of conversations I share with others. As much as possible I surround myself with thoughts and activities that provide a release from fear, because this creates an environment for me to start getting in touch with my unconscious.
- I don't say to myself, 'Now what is it? What are you fearful of?' Rather, I encourage my mind to relax because it is in that relaxed space that the answers come from my unconscious. If I start analysing I am likely to make the situation worse by imagining reasons to fear that are illusionary.

Second, I spend some time on focused activities that encourage me to slip down into my unconscious. In the early morning I write in my journal. This is a time of day when I more easily access my unconscious, where fears from the past are buried. If it is not easy for me to write early in the morning, or if I get the urge to write at other times of the day, that is fine also. I might also draw. These days I ensure I have blank pieces of paper and crayons handy and if I feel the urge, I draw my fears. This can be a powerful way of gaining further insight into my fears, especially after meditating. Drawing seems to sidestep the conscious mind more than writing. My drawings have lots of symbolic images that I spend time 'befriending'. That is, I try not to make quick judgments about what these symbols mean. I spend time with them, 'listening' to what they might be trying to tell me. I come back to the drawings over several days with the same intent. Within a couple of days I have usually gained much insight into my fears. Writing poetry, painting, dancing or any other creative activity that comes to mind can also be ways of gaining access to fears in our unconscious.

TAKE ACTION TO SHOW YOU ARE ABLE TO FACE YOUR FEAR

Once you have identified a fear, take some action to start moving through the fear. To illustrate this point, I will describe the steps I took to work through a fear that had the potential to restrict the way I experienced my life—in this case the celebration of my fiftieth birthday.

One month before turning 50 I started to plan a celebration, but within a week of starting this planning I realised there was an enormous amount of fear in me. At first I didn't understand why I was feeling so anxious. Then while 'sitting with myself' one day I noticed I experienced strong feelings of anxiety every time my fiftieth birthday celebration came to mind. I considered cancelling it. Luckily I first rang Michael Johnson, a wonderful harp player I had booked to come and play at my celebration. I told him about my fears and he explained to me a fear exercise that involved drawing.

When I did my drawing I could see that there were many fears I needed to look at if I was going to celebrate my fiftieth birthday in the way I wanted to. I knew it meant a lot to me to be able to be in an authentic, openly expressive place for my fiftieth birthday celebration. I wanted to feel free to be exactly who I was. A very different me to the one who had been present on my fortieth birthday, when I was experiencing the beginning of my midlife transition as a time of crisis. At that time, without my understanding what was happening to me, I was at that point of choice, knowing I had to start making significant changes in how I was living my life. I experienced much anxiety as I struggled to not show my true feelings at my birthday celebration. Now, leading up to my fiftieth birthday, with unknown fears swirling around inside me I could see I had a lot of work to do. Over the next month I spent much time and energy working through many of these fears. I will now explain to you how I worked with one of them.

In my drawing there was a face smiling, and just hidden behind it was a face crying. After thinking about this part of my drawing over several days I realised I was fearful that when I gave a speech, which I very much wanted to do, I might cry. My rational self told me it didn't matter, friends told me it wouldn't matter; however, the fear remained inside me over the next couple of weeks. For some reason, a few weeks before my birthday the thought of crying in front of all my family and friends seemed catastrophic. It didn't make sense. Most had seen me cry. And my rational self told me it didn't matter to cry in public, especially with friends and family. But still the fear was there. After drawing, I did some writing. And then after much soul-searching and work I came to a personal insight that made all the difference. This insight might not seem much—but for me it was profound and liberating.

While meditating a couple of days before my party a little voice inside me said, 'I cry when I feel deeply'. I had never acknowledged this before. I knew I was increasingly finding it easier to cry in all sorts of situations. I also know that as a young girl I was very much discouraged, and even punished, for crying. But when I thought about my crying in this way I felt a sense of relief. Somebody else could have made this observation and it would not have had the same effect. This understanding had to come from deep inside me. It was an important understanding for me that I had to come to about myself. I now considered what action I could take to incorporate this new insight into my celebration. Was it enough just to know this? I decided it wasn't. What I decided to do was to say at the beginning of my speech, 'I cry when I feel deeply. So if I cry while I am talking today please don't worry. It is only that I am feeling deeply.' Once I made the decision to say this, my fear about crying in front of everybody disappeared.

Somehow the decision to take this action made all the difference. In the process I was acknowledging an important part of myself that until then had been unacknowledged by me all my life—or certainly all of my conscious life. Looking back, as a little girl I cried with ease in many situations that moved me. Over the years I learnt to hide this part of me. Now I decided to consciously acknowledge this part of myself in front of my family and friends.

In working through this fear I can now see there were four steps I needed to take:

1   notice the fear in me
2   gain insight about what was triggering the fear
3   come to an understanding about what from my past was triggering this fear
4   decide on an action to show I could face my fear.

I suggest you try these steps next time you notice a fear arising in you. Once you start facing your fears you will be amazed by how much more fulfilling life becomes as you open up to more of yourself and your own life.

PART 3

Connecting with your story

CHAPTER 10

telling your story

It is in our stories, and in telling them, that we find out who we are.

Arnold Zable

EACH OF US HAS A unique story that we are living every day. All stories have a beginning, a middle and an end and we develop a deeper understanding of our own life when we are able to link these parts of our own story at midlife. As we connect with our stories, including those buried long ago, we awaken different aspects of our Self. This awakening assists us to create a second half of life centred on the person we really are.

We are connecting with our story all the time. Over a lunch break at work a colleague asks: 'How are you, mate?' We arrive home in the evening and are asked, 'How was your day?' We meet a friend for a drink and they ask, 'How's life going?' Given the conditioning many men experienced in the first half of life, such inquiries are unlikely to be met with much self-analysis or self-disclosure. Baby boomer men were encouraged to be emotionally self-contained and to talk about facts and outer events in conversation, rather than about themselves and their inner world. Many men I interviewed expressed a yearning to meaningfully connect with other men at midlife. They also said that despite this need, they found it too difficult to do. If they talked about their innermost thoughts and feelings it tended to be to their female partner, or to some other woman, perhaps a sister, a work colleague, a platonic female friend, or an ex-lover. So, most men I interviewed found it difficult to move out of the old, stereotypical ways of relating to each other. A couple of men I interviewed had joined a men's group, another had joined an encounter group with both men and women, another had joined a men's book group where he felt more comfortable sharing his inner world than in other all-men situations in his life.

We risk the chance to gain any depth of awareness of our own story if we do not take time to examine it. We can connect to our own story while talking to a counsellor, writing in a journal, reading autobiographies or exploring our creativity. As we find ways to get in touch with all the riches of our past, including all the sadness and misfortune, we can grieve for aspects of our life. As we get in touch with forgotten dreams we may need professional help to express unresolved grief and anger. This grieving encourages us to use our remaining time more wisely. For example, in my early forties, while telling my story to a counsellor I started grieving for all the dancing, singing and music I had not allowed in my life. This grieving led me to explore ways to bring them into my life and each are now a regular part of my life. If I hadn't told my story and grieved for my lost opportunities I would not have created these new opportunities. I would have just buried this important part of myself and my second half of life would be significantly less rich.

Choosing a way to connect with your story

You will have automatically started to connect with your own story as you read about other men's stories in earlier chapters. This process will happen faster and deeper if you now take some positive action to connect further with your story. It need not be too formal. You could gather some photos from your life and put them in a series. You could sit in a comfortable chair with a glass of your favourite wine and reflect on your life. You could draw on a large piece of paper or, using images and words, create your story on your computer. If words appeal you could start writing from the beginning of your life, or you could do the same using poetry. Whatever you decide on, I encourage you to make this commitment to yourself.

You don't have to do all the telling before you read on, just try to start in some way now. And, of course, when you have connected with your story it can help the process to have another person listen to your story. If this idea appeals, consider asking your wife, partner or a friend if you could have some time with them to talk about your life. You could ask them if they would like to do the same. If none of this appeals, that's fine. In your own space and time you will find your own way to tell your story.

DIVIDING YOUR STORY INTO SECTIONS CAN MAKE IT EASIER

The thought of writing your whole story can seem quite overwhelming, and to make the task less daunting you can divide your life into sections or chapters and tell it a bit at a time. What are the chapters of your life so far? We can look closely at each chapter. Our initial focus is on the past. As we connect with the personae we have acted out in the first half of life, we can examine them and consider which ones do not reflect who we really are. In sifting through our past we may also come across a forgotten possibility—a forgotten part of our Self. In the past we made choices in preference to other options. If we return to these forks in the road we may now be able to pursue other options.

To start with, you could divide your life into periods of time such as nought to seven years, seven to fourteen years and so on until your present age. Therefore, if you are aged 42 you would have six chunks of time to connect with. You don't want to think about making it a wonderful production, but rather a time of connecting with yourself.

If you feel that by including another in this process you will be self-conscious, just tell yourself your story, or you could tell it to your dog or cat. It doesn't matter. The important thing, as I said before, is just to find a way to tell it, and connect with it.

If you are going to spread the 'telling your story' over a week or several weeks I suggest you choose a particular time of the day. Early morning is often a good time as your mind is fresh and you can easily slip into your unconscious where buried memories lie. If you put aside time every morning for a week you might cover most of your life. Then again, you might need several mornings of writing to cover just one period. Then again you might want to just write when the urge takes you. There is no time constraint, so find what best suits you.

LISTENING TO YOUR STORY

The way you were listened to as a child has a significant effect on your own listening skills, and subsequent development of self-understanding and self-esteem. It can be quite a shock to reach midlife and realise that for much of your life most of your inner thoughts and feelings have gone unheard, including by yourself.

Listening for the feelings

Because most men have been discouraged from developing either the habit of feeling or a language in which to express it, a significant part of midlife transition for many men focuses on their emotional development. They need to work hard if they are to recreate the emotional freedom of the boy within—the boy who cried when he got hurt, who yelled his joy when he won a game, or freely hugged his family and friends. This does not mean that at midlife you need to become childish or childlike. At first the behaviours may feel unfamiliar; however, gradually as layer after layer is peeled away to expose the feeling core, this part of you will be integrated into your understanding of Self.

Many men have been conditioned to listen for facts and details. These men will have difficulty listening to feelings expressed explicitly or implicitly. If you are one of these men, you can now train yourself to focus more on feelings, both in your conversations with others, and in how you listen to yourself. Then you will be taking a significant step towards improving your communication skills. When listening at a feeling level to another there can be a tendency, especially in your eagerness to demonstrate this new skill, to sound like a mind-reader. For example, you may be tempted to respond, 'You are angry'. It is preferable to make your reflective response tentative, such as, 'It sounds as if you are angry'. The person might come back with, 'No, I'm not angry, just disappointed'. Even if your understanding is wrong, by putting it tentatively you give the speaker the invitation to correct you. They know you are trying to understand. They feel listened to.

So, before you listen to your own or another's story, reflect on your own listening behaviour. Are you ready to listen to these stories with an open, compassionate, attentive, non-judgmental mind? This is what is necessary. To go to this place of sharing is to go to a place of trust. We make ourselves very vulnerable as we share our innermost feelings and thoughts and it is vital that we hold these feelings and thoughts in a safe place, whether for ourself or another. For many of us this can be a unique experience as we are listened to in a way we have never experienced before.

A listening exercise

During my years of consulting to corporations I often facilitated a listening exercise to help others reflect on their own listening behaviour and their own experiences around being listened to. I have listed some of the questions from this exercise. You might like to ask them of yourself.

- *Think of someone who does not seem to listen to you. What does this person do to make you feel he or she is not listening to you?*
- *How do you feel when speaking to them?*
- *Think of a person who listens to you well. What do they do to show they are listening to you?*
- *How do you feel when talking to them?*
- *Think of a time recently when you did not listen effectively to somebody important in your life. What happened?*

These questions helped clients focus on their own experiences around listening, and the behaviours and attitudes that create an effective listening environment. I would then talk about how our listening experiences as a young child with parents, teachers and significant others shaped our own listening behaviour. If we were not listened to when young, it is unlikely that we would have these skills now, unless we have consciously learnt them.

Some important listening behaviours and attitudes that were identified as a result of this exercise were: emptying one's mind of other matters, eye contact, facing the person, giving them your full attention, keeping an open mind—not judging the storyteller, and not interrupting and then taking over the conversation. After listening well it was appropriate for the listener to check that they had understood correctly by reflecting back the feelings and thoughts they heard.

Broaden your feeling vocabulary

Because men often lack experience in being listened to at a feeling level, or in dealing with their own or others' feelings, they tend not to have developed a wide vocabulary when exploring and explaining their feelings. When asked how he feels, a man's most common response will be 'good', 'fine' or 'not too bad'. The 'Table of feeling words' at the end of this chapter lists some words, indicating varying degrees of feeling. How many of these words would you use with ease when describing your own or another's feelings?

Feel your emotions

Another tendency can be that once a man has learnt to describe his feelings, that is where it ends. It is not enough for us to know our feelings, we also need to allow ourself to experience them. So as you connect with your story, endeavour to connect at an emotional level with the feelings evoked, not just at a descriptive, thinking level.

First learn to listen to yourself

We can only show to another the attitudes we show to ourself, and so when developing your listening skills an important starting place is to attend to your own story with a 'listening' ear. You might like to try to use some of the feeling words listed in the table to describe your experiences. You could even put your story on a tape and then listen to it, as though it was another's, and then think about what questions you would ask to clarify some of the underlying feelings and thoughts.

Are you ready to commit to listening to your own story? I hope so. From my experience, as we start seeing the threads in our own story at midlife, we can take the experiences from our past into the present, and then into our future. With these threads we are then able to create a rich tapestry for the second half of our life.

THREE DIFFERENT WAYS TO TELL YOUR STORY

In the following three chapters we will explore three different methods you could use to tell your story. Michael's story demonstrates these three different processes. Chapter 11 illustrates how he used the 'turning points' exercise to explore his first half of life. Then in Chapter 12 you can see how he explored his time of 'midlife crisis' through poetry. And in Chapter 13 you can see how he used intuitive drawing to explore his time of midlife transition.

You don't need to use any of these methods. You can use one of the other ones suggested at the beginning of this chapter, or you can create your own. It is up to you.

Table of feeling words

	Feeling states				
	Angry	**Sad**	**Confused**	**Joyful**	**Frightened**
Strong	furious	sorrowful	bewildered	euphoric	terrified
	mad	bereft	lost	ecstatic	horrified
	livid	dejected	fogged	radiant	afraid
	ropeable	depressed	trapped	elated	fearful
Medium	annoyed	unhappy	disorganised	bright	nervous
	upset	glum	befuddled	cheerful	apprehensive
	agitated	deflated	bemused	happy	scared
	riled	despondent	baffled	excited	insecure
Weak	irritated	flat	muddled	pleased	anxious
	cross	bad	uncertain	contented	timid
	put out	low	puzzled	good	uneasy
	dismayed	down	dithery	glad	unsure

CHAPTER 11

storytelling through turning points

Each of us carries a unique world within our hearts—each soul
is a different shape. No one feels your life as you do; no one
experiences things the way you do. Your life is a totally
unique story and only you really know it from within.

John O'Donohue, *Anam Cara—Spiritual Wisdom from the Celtic World*

ONE WAY TO WRITE your story is to use 'turning points'. I suggest you pick up to twelve turning points in your life so far and then use them to connect different periods of your life. Or you can use this exercise by taking a particular period of your life that you wish to explore. To demonstrate this process we first read Michael's interview where he describes the first half of his life. He then lists twelve turning points from this time.

Michael's story—from the first half of life

I grew up in a small town in Austria and I was the second child of two. My sister was eleven years older so I really didn't have much contact with her. At one and a half I had an accident which shaped my life profoundly. My face was burned. It happened when I was home with grandma. She was preparing the traditional Sunday lunch while my parents were at church. She was lifting the roast pan and the boiling gravy spilt over my head when the handle slipped. I was in hospital struggling with my life for a few weeks because of blood poisoning following the accident and, of course, because I was only a year and a half old. That was in my unconscious memory. It is only in the past ten years that I have dug a bit more into my childhood, and have realised how deep an impact that event had on my life. Feeling abandoned by my parents, being in a hospital with my hands and feet tied down because otherwise I would scratch my terribly burned face. And I think the adults lied to me and said I would be home tomorrow, I would be out soon and so on and so that left a deep mark on me.

My childhood otherwise I remember as easygoing. My father was a carpenter. There wasn't very much money around but we had our own home. There was always enough there anyway. It was a very religious upbringing. Also lots of good memories of playing with the boys and doing all sorts of fun things. I remember I was a bit embarrassed by my father. Because of some driver's licence regulations, he could only drive vehicles up to a certain motor size. And so at the beginning we had a motorcycle and then when I was seven he bought a small car. It was a very small car and I felt embarrassed about it. At that time I became determined that I would have lots of money in my life and would have a big car.

I was sick quite a bit, mainly tonsillitis. My tonsils came out at some stage but it continued on. Being sick was a good way to get attention from my mother. She gave me good food that otherwise I wouldn't get—special fruit and things. I realised later on how much I unconsciously used this way to get attention. I was very good at school and I started earning money from an early age. I was probably eight when I started to do a paper round and distribute leaflets, earning a few dollars and buying my own stuff because my pocket money was not very generous.

I had to fight for my education. The school system was such that at class four or five you had to make a decision as to whether you would continue to the basic primary stream or whether you would go to the mid stream or the high school stream. It was a fairly big decision that could influence my life. So at ten years old when this decision came up, my father was ill and he wanted me to go through school as quickly as possible and earn some money. I realised that wasn't what I wanted to do so I got my teachers to go home to my parents and have a good talk with them. Somehow, I knew that I didn't want to stay there, and I wasn't prepared to just let it go by. And that worked out well. So they allowed me to go into the middle stream, and that gave me the opportunity then, three or four years later, to change to the high school stream. That was a big move, coming from a lower socioeconomic background. Very few of my mates actually got into the high school stream. That separated me a little bit from the rest but I had new friends at the new school so it didn't worry me.

The onset of sexuality hit me fairly hard. I took a great interest in it and I actually again earned some money. I got a book about sexuality with some pictures in it, not a porno book, but some good information and I hired it out, and I charged by the day. That was an interesting time. We had lots of talks among us boys and also some innocent orgies. We would occasionally masturbate in a group. Great fun actually. So there was a lot of stuff on sex floating around.

At fourteen I got a great holiday job. I always had jobs during holidays to make some money to buy the clothes I wanted, a bike and all sort of things I wouldn't get from my parents. I was lucky enough to get a job that today you would call a computer operator in a manufacturing company. And back then there were only two computers in my town, so I was very lucky. And so I earned good money and I also got an insight into how manufacturing organisations work, which was part of my career for the next 30 years. I had a role model there whom you would probably call a mentor. He was the general manager and he impressed me a lot. Everybody had great respect for him. He was a great guy. Everybody looked up to him. He had power. He had money and a big house and a big car. He was my role model.

I had my first girlfriend when I was sixteen and that went for about three years. We quite liked each other but I came to a point when I realised I had to move on. I suppose I stuffed up everything you could stuff up in ending that relationship.

For the six weeks before turning eighteen I had a car waiting outside our house. I had bought it myself. The car was standing there in front of the house waiting for me to get a licence and it was a much bigger car than my father's. Nothing outrageous, but just a good car. I had been working for a long time and I had my own money. I was doing very well at the time and so then I was able to drive to school. The car became very important to me. During my final year in school, I realised I wanted to get away from where I lived. It was a university town and although I originally wanted to study chemistry, it would have meant I would have had to study at home. The next best choice was business administration and I went to another university town to study this.

I realised I had to do something to join a different social life and I decided I would join a student fraternity. It was quite a big step because I didn't have the same background as the others. But I got in there and it meant all sorts of things like fencing and doing all sorts of crazy stuff. I suppose from a man's point of view I see it as an initiation ritual. You actually had to risk your blood, your body for the fraternity and there were some serious mandatory fights there with sword-like weapons. You had to fight in order to just belong. I didn't quite see the point of it, but it was an initiation ritual and in that respect it allowed me to get into that sphere. I took responsibility for various positions within the fraternity for some years and it taught me how to behave at these levels.

And at the same time I was working and earning lots of money, as well as studying. As a student I was driving brand new cars, had lots of friends, lots of drinking. The fraternity had beer drinking contests. It meant you got drunk fairly regularly, at least once or twice a week. I made great friends there. During that time, money, cars, booze and women were my focus in life. I also studied and that came fairly easily.

I then decided it would be good for widening my horizon to spend a year in America. I don't know how I managed it but somehow I got a scholarship from a company to pay for me to go over there for a year. So I spent a year at a university doing the minimum of study in order to keep the scholarship going. I wanted to get to know a different country. I travelled a lot and had a great time. That was a wonderful experience that expanded my horizon. I had great difficulties when I came back. That was a time of my life when I floundered most.

While in the States I fell in love with a great woman and I had difficulties letting go. Back home everything seemed so small, and for six months I was really struggling and drinking a lot and then somehow I pulled myself out of it. And that's when I met my wife. She represented a totally different dimension of life from what I had experienced so far, with all the arts and music in particular, and painting, literature and nature. That's where she was at home. For me this type of world hadn't existed before. There had just been stupid things like cars, booze and women and having fun. I was attracted to getting to know these parts of myself. I sensed there was something I had completely missed up until that time. I completed my studies and she became pregnant and that was quite okay with me. We got married and I started a career, doing the normal thing working 60 or 70 hours a week. These working hours were quite normal as I was establishing myself. I was very successful and got lots of rewards for it. But I neglected my wife and kids. My work was my main focus and I didn't see much of them. My wife made it clearly understood that that wasn't okay and I tried but I couldn't combine it properly.

At the end of my twenties a favourite aunty died and it affected me strongly. I started to open myself up to look at all the religions from a different perspective to what I had experienced when young. I went searching for answers to some fairly basic questions and considered the purpose of life. It was at this time that for whatever reason, I felt drawn to Australia. My wife was quite settled. We had a beautiful house and everything was going well. I didn't want to go to the States. I lived there for a year, and I realised that was a great time, but I didn't want to live there. New Zealand was my first choice, but I then enquired about visas and they were fairly rude. The Australians were rude too, but less than the New Zealanders were. I'll never know exactly the reasons for wanting to come here. I had a bit of difficulty because I wanted to go and my wife really didn't want to. So we decided to come out here for a holiday and I loved it and it was okay with her. It was really me sort of going for it and I said, 'Okay, why don't we try it out, and if we don't like it, we go back'. The kids were six and three at the time.

As this was going on I was told out of the blue—I was about thirty at the time—that I had an hereditary disease in one eye. I was told I would go blind in that eye very quickly and there was a good chance it would happen in the other eye as well. The doctor said, 'Sorry mate, nothing we can do, but at least you have computing skills. We send our blind people into computing'. That pulled the whole rug out from underneath my values system, having fun and having money and having power and just enjoying life. There was no room for blindness.

That was at the time when I was thinking of coming here. And before that, I had been thinking about religion but I didn't follow it up. I dabbled in it. I read a bit here and a bit there. When this professor told me the shocking news about my sight, in that split second I knew it actually had to do with my search for some answers to these fundamental questions. And subsequently I changed my life profoundly to give much more focus to looking at these questions of life and reading a lot and contemplating a lot and I started to meditate.

Four months after that I thought, 'Oh well, maybe I'll get a second opinion and get more information about the illness'. And I was then told when I did the test again that the infection in the eye had come to a standstill. And so the risk of going blind had disappeared for the time being. And so that pressure was taken off. It was very interesting to live for four months with that sort of understanding and it has changed my life. I didn't go back to the old style of living after the diagnosis was changed.

I developed a very dedicated spiritual life alongside my career. I meditated, read, studied and contemplated a lot during that time. It changed my life profoundly. Then after that diagnosis was changed, it became very clear that we should come here to Australia and my wife said, okay, she was willing to join in with it. So we packed our bags and came out here. We didn't know anybody and I didn't want to know anybody. I liked the challenge of just starting from scratch and setting up something new. I applied for jobs and within two weeks I had a job with a large manufacturing company. I didn't quite know what I was getting into, I just wanted a job. I didn't understand the Aussie slang. And so we settled the kids, we rented a house for six months and then bought one close to the children's school.

Michael's twelve turning points from the first half of his life

1. (1 year) Had an accident where half my face was burned. Was hospitalised for several weeks. Felt abandoned by parents. At midlife realised it had affected me greatly.
2. (8 years) Started to do a paper round. Earned my first money.
3. (10 years) Got teachers to talk to my parents so I could go to the school I wanted to. Meant I could have the education I wanted.
4. (14 years) Started getting very interested in sex. Got a book about sexuality with pictures and hired it out.
5. (15 years) School holiday job with manufacturing company. Ended up working with manufacturing companies for 30 years.
6. (16 years) First girlfriend.
7. (18 years) First car bought from my own money.
8. (19 years) Joined student fraternity—my entrée into a different social life.
9. (20 years) Spent a year in America on a scholarship. Loved being in a different country and travelling.
10. (22 years) Met my wife.
11. (30 years) Told I would go blind then four months later that I wouldn't. Started questioning everything. Started my spiritual journey.
12. (32 years) Came to Australia with family and started work.

FINDING YOUR TURNING POINTS

Can you see how these twelve turning points connect with Michael's story from the first half of his life? Now that you have read this example, I suggest you use this approach for a period of life you want to understand better. To get into the right frame of mind I suggest you close your eyes, then focus your attention on the period of life you wish to connect with. After several minutes open your eyes, take a pen and quickly jot down the turning points that come to mind. Don't do too much thinking. Work as intuitively as possible. You can then use the turning points you have listed (it doesn't have to be twelve) to write about your story, or the period of your life you want to explore. Once you have your list of turning points, you can link them with narrative and in the process you are starting to write the story of your life.

CHAPTER 12

storytelling through poetry

Poetry deals with powerful emotions recollected in tranquillity.

William Wordsworth, *Lyrical Ballads and Related Writings*

CONNECTING WITH SOME of your story through poetry may seem daunting at first. However, it is worth attempting as it can be a very quick route to capturing aspects of your story in a vivid way. As you express in just a few words what you have experienced you can gain new insights into emotions and recollections buried long ago. When you have decided what you want to write about, it is important to tune in to the experience through all your senses—through your whole being.

WRITING POETRY

Recently I attended a course where several times during the day we were asked to write some poetry about what we had just experienced. When we were first asked to do this I became anxious, thinking back to school days of trying to make everything rhyme. Of course, there are many poems that do rhyme, but I quickly realised this was not necessary. When you are writing a poem it is important not to sacrifice meaning for rhyme. Your poem should say exactly what you want it to. The best way of all to write poetry is to just do it. Let the natural poetry of your soul and heart flow onto the page. To show you what I mean, some well-known excerpts of poetry that could be seen as meaningful representations of aspects of midlife are given below.

> If he closes off every passage way
> And escape route
> It's because he wants to show you
> A secret way which no one knows.
> —Rumi

> Two roads diverged in a yellow wood,
> And sorry I could not travel both
> And be one traveller, long I stood
> And looked down one as far as I could
> To where it bent in the undergrowth
> —Robert Frost, *The Road Not Taken*

> Midway this way of life we're bound upon,
> I woke to find myself in a dark wood,
> Where the right road was wholly lost and gone.
> —Dante, *The Divine Comedy*

> In the silence
> Let us listen
> To our heart
> —Michael Leunig, *Common Prayer Collection*

> Be ye lamps unto yourselves,
> Be your own reliance
> Hold on to the truth within yourselves
> As to the only lamp
> —Buddha

One day you finally knew
what you had to do, and began,
though the voices around you
kept shouting
their bad advice . . .
    —Mary Oliver, *The Journey*

In this chapter Michael describes his time of 'midlife crisis'—that is his point of choice—whether or not he would stay in his old life or move on. Once you have read Michael's description and some examples of short verse that represent this time of his life, I suggest you try to write some poetry of your own.

Michael's time of midlife crisis

By my early forties, I had responsibility for the business side of a large manufacturing company. I enjoyed it. But I then hit a midlife crisis. I was in my early forties and I was even lecturing about the stages of life, including the midlife crisis. And I thought I knew it all and I thought, 'This wasn't meant to happen to me'. It hit me from a totally unexpected angle.

Something I had relied on all my life, which I had absolutely taken for granted, suddenly wasn't so available anymore. All my life, if there was a challenge at work or a challenge anywhere, I just rolled up my sleeves a bit more and charged forward. And I had the ability to take 100 or 200 people with me on that journey. I never thought about it, it was just me. And I came to a point when I realised I was running out of puff and I was running out of strength and that thing which I had taken for granted wasn't unlimited. And that scared the hell out of me. I just realised that I didn't have the energy anymore and I got ill. I got heart and digestive problems and insomnia. And that in a way paralysed me for a year or two. Up until then I knew so clearly where my life was going, no worries. Clear priorities, clear goals, and suddenly that all fell in a heap. I didn't know where I was going.

The business was floundering and we were making losses and people were saying, 'Where are we going?' I remember these staff meetings. Fair enough, they wanted to know where we were going and I was standing there with my back against the wall and I didn't know where we were going. I felt like crying. I had to prop myself up against the wall and pretend that I knew and deep down I was just lost. I felt numb. I had to pretend. Doing all sorts of things really. Getting fairly uptight about things and using raw power to push and change things. I was desperate . . . there was fear, I was driven by fear. I had a fantastic run up until then and I had a lot of freedom to do things the way I wanted to do it because the results were there. But when that had changed, I got under a fair amount of pressure as you normally do.

I remember one devastating experience. I had a friend who was an organisational consultant and I got him to interview the senior people who reported directly to me. I asked him to just do a bit of a survey of how they felt, how the business was going, and what was happening in the different departments. When he reported back in summary form, it was a mirror image of where I was at. And for me that was so shocking because at that moment I realised the whole thing was not going to change until I changed. As the senior person, as the boss, I set the scene. As long as I was floundering and was lost, the business would be lost. I felt a tremendous pressure on me. There was nothing in a way they could do, until I changed. And that was the low point. And then two months later somehow I managed to cut through, to turn the corner inwardly and I found there was life after this. I found that I could tap into a different resource, a different energy source. At the time I wasn't very clear about it. I'm much clearer now. But I just got a sense that I had to trust. I had a very strong spiritual life. I was actively lecturing about connections with the spiritual world, but to apply it to my own life wasn't so easy.

I had a choice. Everybody has a choice to either operate out of fear or out of trust and by operating out of fear, I tried to control things and I was running out of energy to control more and more things and so I just realised well, I have a choice there. I started to actually like the choice and just be more relaxed about things. So I came to a place where I was more trusting, not being uptight about things. I was still working very hard, but I had a different attitude towards it. And I think it was also the time when I formed a decision that I would leave, so this detached me a bit from my work. For six months I was actively working with that decision to leave the business world. And then within six months the business picked up tremendously, things were changing and that was at a time when things were going well, when I realised that I wanted to get out. I wanted to get out before but I just could not leave while things were in a mess. At 43 I decided it was time to leave. It was tempting to stay there because things were going well. I'd think, 'I'll just stay for another year to get the benefits and so on', but I decided it was time to go. I had the big house, the big car, I had lots of money and it just left me absolutely flat.

It was difficult because my wife made it very clear she was not in favour of me leaving the business world. It was just not on that I would leave because I didn't know what I would want to do afterwards. I just knew I had to leave. And I couldn't say for how long. I had enough money put aside to keep the family going for a year or longer, school fees and everything, so outwardly not much would have changed. Maybe a bit less holidays and so on, but nothing substantial. I was also very clear I wouldn't sit on my backside for the rest of my life and do nothing. But I just needed to let go.

I was clear that I wouldn't go back into the same environment. And that just brought out too much fear in my wife. But I was very clear, I needed to be true to my values and it was really based on values. I couldn't see that I would use my life energy to prop up a system which from my perspective had deadly flaws built into it. To contribute to maximise the performance for shareholders in a public company was too hollow for me. And that is really what it boils down to. If you work in a public company, a publicly listed company, shareholders' performance counts. And the rest is fairly secondary. So I just had to be true to myself and leave. And so that meant that we would separate and we just worked out it was easier for me to leave the house than for her.

Below are suggestions for some short verses that encapsulate Michael's story. You could then use the 'Steps for writing poetry' guidelines given after these verses to help you get started on your own creation of short verse.

Some short verses about Michael's time of midlife crisis

Midlife crisis
Panic, business losing money, going downhill
Failure. I feel like a total loser.

I am exhausted, my will runs out of steam
More control, desperate use of power
My back to the wall. Paralysed. Fear

Fog all over the valley
Panic efforts to clear the fog
The fog closes in even more

I cannot hold it any longer
I am ready for the ultimate punishment of failure—
Black, humiliating death

Transformed the fog
A beautiful valley breathing in the warmth of spring
A miracle—I grasp the meaning of trust and warmth for my life

Steps for writing poetry

Now it is your turn. You may like to use the following steps to start yourself off.

- *Take a pen and something to write on.*
- *Find a quiet spot where you won't be interrupted.*
- *Sit quietly for about ten minutes, preferably with your eyes closed; still your mind.*
- *After approximately ten minutes, tune into the experience in your life that you would like to write about.*
- *Connect with that experience through all your senses.*

When you feel you are ready, open your eyes and start to write. You can write some short verses or a longer one. Whatever you decide to write, don't judge your work. Know that these words need only be for your own eyes.

CHAPTER 13

storytelling through intuitive drawing

*Explore the unknown. Creation leads you to the longing of
your heart and soul. Every stream flows towards the ocean.*

Michele Cassou, *Point Zero: Creativity Without Limits*

MANY OF US WHO were schoolchildren in the 1950s and 1960s
had very unimaginative experiences in exploring drawing. In this
chapter I am not encouraging you to create a beautiful drawing. In
fact, that is probably the last thing I want you to focus on. The aim of
drawing here is to encourage you to slip down into your unconscious
where forgotten memories and insights lie. If you allow yourself to be
relaxed as you draw, the process tends to bypass your intellect. This
leads more easily to your unconscious and in the process you create
an intuitive drawing.

DRAWING IS A TOOL FOR SELF-UNDERSTANDING

At the age of 47 I had a powerful experience in a workshop titled,
'Bringing Your Story to Life', when I was asked to create a drawing.
As a result of this experience I have continued to use drawing in my

everyday life as a tool for Self-understanding. I have found it a very powerful way to access my unconscious, even more so than writing. At any time before I attended this workshop, if anybody asked me to draw, I just froze. Now I find that if I follow certain guidelines it is a very easy place for me to go to.

Guidelines for creating an intuitive drawing

- Gather together some materials such as several large pieces of white drawing paper, oil pastels and markers of various colours and a pencil.
- Set aside some time.
- Find a quiet spot where there are no distractions. Check you have turned off your telephone.
- Spend ten minutes in quiet contemplation about a particular part of your life.
- As you start to draw, reassure yourself that this drawing is just for you.
- When finished, don't judge it. Put it in a place where you can look at it from time to time. You may be surprised at some of the memories it evokes.

I will now recount the experiences I had as I attended the workshop as I think my experience illustrates how drawing can assist us at midlife to connect with our story.

We were asked to spend ten minutes drawing our main home as a child. Any 'draw-a-phobes' are no doubt experiencing the same feelings I had at the thought of this. I tried to draw the roof-line of our large, rambling, Victorian, weatherboard home. After a couple of minutes I realised this wasn't what we were meant to be focusing on. I went for it. It was no work of art. Memories came flooding back. I remembered times spent in our large garden. Memories came to me of a hollow bush where I would go to be alone and dream.

I drew the rose bushes I loved to smell, especially after school. It helped me to relax. I placed my family in our home. Where to put them? What were they doing? I didn't think too much. My pencil flew over the large piece of paper as more and more memories came flooding back.

We were asked in turn to talk about our drawings. Each picture held many stories. When it was my turn, I got up to speak. I said, 'I lived in this home from the age of two to seventeen years. It was my only childhood home. I left it at seventeen, just after my mother died.' I then went to a place I had never been to before. In the years of counselling I had talked at times about my mother's illness and subsequent death, but had never been able to contact the feelings that I knew were buried very deep inside. I did now; not for long—perhaps for a minute. Nobody said or did anything. I am so thankful for that. I collected up my feelings. I continued to show the drawing of my childhood home.

I got home that night feeling absolutely drained. I still had very sad feelings washing over me. For homework we were asked to prepare a collage to represent the passing of our childhood. Up until this time in my adult life, when I thought of my childhood I could usually only remember the negative aspects. I knew this wasn't the truth. All those unresolved, sad feelings from my mother's illness and death had flowed out over my childhood. As I sat at home that night and prepared my collage I realised I was focusing on positive aspects. I was remembering my childhood differently.

The rest of this chapter records Michael's description of his time of midlife transition and then a drawing he did about this time. Remember, it is not about creating a work of art, it is about evoking memories and insights, often from deep within your unconscious.

Michael's time of midlife transition

I went from a very highly paid job with all the perks to living in a small commune. There were very simple living conditions—growing our own vegetables and going into the bush to chop some firewood if we wanted to be warm. So I simplified my lifestyle completely and I had time to do all the things which I had never had time to do before. I enjoyed it. It was very painful with the separation from the family; however, I did see my two sons regularly. I had lots of support from the people in the commune and good friends. I thought it would only take me a year but after a year I didn't have a clue what I should be doing. During this year I was doing some volunteer work and I started a counselling course. I also explored my creativity. I enjoyed life to the full. I got a bit nervous at times because I felt I should know what I should be doing. I tried a few things but they didn't work and so I just let myself be.

During that period I had a lot of time to do inner work. After my midlife crisis I had to do a lot of work regarding my mother and my father. It was a bit difficult because they were on the other side of the world but I did a lot of work inwardly. I realised that I didn't have an easy relationship with my masculinity and I started to look at the relationship with my mother. I realised that she had filtered, coloured, the way I saw my father. I never really saw my father. I only saw him through the eyes of my mother and he did not score well in her eyes. Yet he was quite a reasonable man. There were lots of problems there and she always told me the same story, what he had done to her and so on. And I took on a bit of guilt and shame about being a man. And that influenced my relationship with my own masculinity.

I was quite influenced at the time by the book *Iron John* by Robert Bly. There was one scene in there which spoke to me a lot. It is about the man freeing himself from the mother. At some stage he had to steal the key from underneath the mother's pillow and that's what I needed to do. After a while I went back to Austria with the clear purpose that I needed to do that. My mother is a very simple person and I couldn't talk about these things with her in this way. But I needed to approach her with a different attitude. She always gave me gifts, she always gave me money. She always looked after me, like when I was ill as a kid, she gave me extra food. I just needed to tell her that I would be quite happy to listen to her if she wanted to talk to me about my father but I would not take these things on anymore. I kept it right out there. She didn't understand what I was talking about. It didn't matter but she felt my different attitude and it made a huge difference to me.

After I returned to Australia I came to a very interesting point. I felt this urge to go at night to this lake near where I lived and I didn't know what was going on. I just had that urge. I needed to dive in and swim in the lake in the middle of the night. It was a strange thing to do. It was a place where we went swimming during summer. It was very muddy and you would sink over the ankles into the mud you stepped in. To go into such a lake at night didn't appeal much to me, I must say. So I took a few mates with me and we had a bit of fun and scared the hell out of ourselves, swimming in it late at night. Eventually I had to go there alone. Nobody knew I was going. And I had to swim out at midnight, and I had to dive down into the water and touch the bottom. And that pressed all the buttons I had. That was the scariest thing for me to do. I didn't like that sort of water, to actually dive down through the different temperature layers. But the moment I touched the bottom, I touched my masculinity. Somehow I made peace with my masculinity.

A few months later I went back to my parents' home again and I met my father in a way I had never met him before and I could listen to him. He told me his childhood stories. He grew up during the wars. He had quite a story to tell and it was the first time I could see him as a person. It was wonderful; it allowed me to make peace. And again that had quite an impact on me and my sexuality. It fitted in with making peace with that part of me which was not at peace before. That was a lot of hard work in a way, but it was so rewarding. And in the last few years I have done work with the inner child.

Now I'm determined to stay in touch with that inner child because for me it's much more than making peace with my childhood. It's actually the fact that the inner child has got all the qualities of innocence, of trust, playfulness and being absorbed in the present, and these are the qualities I want to nurture in life. It also helps me in reconnecting with the spiritual world which is there for every child but as a child grows older, that gate closes, and when they become an adult, usually that gate is bolted.

So over the past four years, I have worked a lot to bring my little boy out. If the little boy disappears into hiding, I'm just acting out old patterns and that's not what I want to do. And so if I know I've lost him—which I may notice in a change in bodily sensation or a change in mood—I make a commitment to him and it won't be long before I go looking for him. I'll maybe go for a walk if that is possible. The absolute latest will be the next morning because I meditate every morning to tune in to this sort of stuff. I go back and say, 'Okay, hey, what happened?' And that happens fairly frequently, but that's okay and then we find each other and off we go. So it helps me to be present, and to know when I'm not present.

My aim is to be open and not needing to protect myself. It also means I have to be vulnerable. Children are very vulnerable, but I know if I get hurt—and I do get hurt of course—it doesn't take me long and I can come back out again. The fear of getting hurt is not an excuse for not being open. I don't want to pretend, though, for any moment that I have got it all together.

Michael's drawing

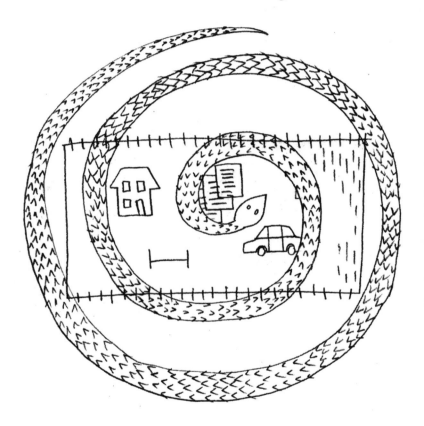

PART 4

Balancing your canoe

CHAPTER 14

self-empowering skills
for creating balance

Make room for yourself in your life by keeping it simple.

Stephen C. Paul, *Illuminations: Visions for Change,*
Growth and Self-acceptance

IF WE ARE TO STEER through all the inevitable difficulties we encounter as we navigate the river of our life we need on board some self-empowering skills to help us on our way. Through my work with clients and through my own midlife journey I have come to the conclusion that there are four vital self-empowering skills for navigating this time of life. These skills help you to simplify your life, assert your self, create self-supporting thoughts, and nurture your self.

MEANINGFUL SIMPLICITY

Once you start navigating the river of your life you need to discard baggage and simplify. Simplifying is not about getting rid of everything you've worked hard for. It's about deciding what's most important to you, and gradually letting go of the things that aren't. What may signify a simple life to you may be very different to what signifies a simple life for someone else. Simplicity is a relative concept. It is also a very personal one.

Your fantasies can be a strong guide for you when simplifying at midlife; however, it is important to look to them for their symbolic, inner meaning rather than to always take them literally. So notice your fantasies and daydreams, and attempt a change in your present situation in the light of this inner meaning. For example, if you have a fantasy to live in the bush it doesn't necessarily mean you need to sell up and buy a bush block. It might mean this, but it is important to ask yourself what it is about this fantasy that is attractive to you. You could consider incorporating these attributes into your present lifestyle. If the answer is that you have a yearning to spend more time outside in touch with nature or by yourself where you have a sense of space, further ask yourself how you can create this time for yourself now.

'Meaningful simplicity' is not necessarily about following our fantasies to 'a hut in the bush'. Many people have left everything behind only to find that it's not necessarily simpler or what suits them. Tempting as it might be at times, acting on our fantasies and escaping our present, complicated life is not the only way to create a simpler life. Meaningful simplicity is about knowing what you most value in life and ensuring that the life you are creating honours these values. Once we put into practice the principles of meaningful simplicity we start to create the life we want to live without escaping to our fantasy world.

Exercises to make meaningful simplicity part of your life

It may help you to do a visualisation or an intuitive drawing to help you tap into what your life might be like if you incorporated the principles of meaningful simplicity into it. Imagine what your life could be like if it was simpler, without making radical changes such as changing your job, place of living or significant relation-ships. Find a quiet, relaxing place where you won't be interrupted and sit or lie and close your eyes. With your mind focused on what this life might be like, see what images come to you. You might get just one image or many images may come flooding in. You can practise this exercise any time of the day—a bit like daydreaming.

Another suggestion is to get some paper and crayons and, holding the thought of what a simpler life might look like for you, see what images come up as you draw. When I did this exercise in my late thirties I drew symbolic images that represented time with my partner, nature, music, dance and writing, none of which were in my life to a great extent at that stage. As I write this I can now see how these images represented aspects of my Self which I needed to bring into my life to make it more personally meaningful. As we realise what is personally meaningful, we want to make time for it. This encourages us to discard those things and activities that are no longer satisfying—an important step in simplifying our life.

Questioning

We can also support ourself in the simplifying process by asking some key questions:

- *What are my top four or five priorities in life? (Chapter 20 on values clarification should assist you here.)*
- *If I simplify my life using these priorities as a guide, what will it look like? What will it feel like?*
- *What do I need to remove from my life in order to simplify it?*
- *What will I gain by making my life simpler?*
- *Once I have simplified my life, how can I ensure it does not become complicated again?*
- *Can I make some easy changes right now or do I have to make some significant changes first?*

Do whatever you need to do to create the personal space to focus on these exercises. You may be able to find some reflective time at home or work. However, most of us need to get right away from our everyday environment to feel free of distractions. Creating this reflective time to focus on bringing meaningful simplicity into your life can be a major turning point at midlife.

ASSERTIVENESS

Once we become more aware of what we do and don't want in our life, we want to be able to express our wishes to others. With ease can you say, 'No' to another when you know what is being requested of you is not one of your priorities? If you find this difficult to do, you might be one of the many people who need to learn to refine their assertiveness skills.

When I became a consultant to organisations in my mid-thirties, one of my first assignments was to design and run an assertiveness course. As I read about assertiveness I was shocked to realise that much of the time I wasn't assertive, especially in my personal life. Since that time I have come to accept that most of us who grew up in the 1950s and 1960s rarely saw assertiveness skills modelled when we were young. As a result many of us reach midlife lacking these skills. We might use them in some situations but this is more often by luck than by conscious choice. Assertiveness is a vital interpersonal skill at midlife if we are to express who we really are. It is also essential if we are to create a second half of life that reflects this new understanding of who we are.

As you read some of the understandings I have found useful in developing my own assertive behaviour, consider how assertive you are in both your personal and professional life.

Important understandings for developing assertiveness

You can create an assertive statement by using these three steps:

- *Step 1*   *Show you understand the other person's perspective.*
- *Step 2*   *Say how you are feeling or thinking.*
- *Step 3*   *Say what you want to happen.*

For example, when your boss asks you to stay back one Friday night you might say: 'I realise you need some help in getting this proposal done (Step 1), *however, I promised my partner I'd get home on time tonight* (Step 2) *and so I'd appreciate it if you could ask somebody else to stay back* (Step 3).'*

- *Assertive behaviour enables us to express our own feelings, thoughts and wishes while at the same time respecting the right of others to do the same. For example, the boss in the above example might respond that there isn't anybody else who can give them the support they need. To be assertive we need to respect their right to respond in this way.*

- *Being assertive doesn't necessarily mean we get our wishes met. An aggressive person is more likely to get their needs met; however, this is often at the expense of their relationships. For example, despite having expressed your wish to not stay back, your boss might become aggressive, saying you have to. They get their way, but your relationship is badly affected.*

- *In contrast to an aggressive person, a passive person rarely gets their needs met because they never make them known. For example, if you were passive in the above example, you would not say anything to your boss in the first place, although you more than likely would have angry feelings inside. When unexpressed these feelings can lead to ill health, poor sense of wellbeing and even depression. When you eventually get home you might also take out these feelings on your partner and children, who are an easier, but inappropriate target for your unexpressed feelings.*

- *Even if we do not get what we want, when we are assertive we behave in a way that means we come away from situations feeling good about ourself. We feel more confident and have the satisfaction that we did not let ourself down, nor did we abuse the rights of others. We show respect for ourself, while at the same time maintaining respect for others. For example, whether or not you end up staying back you will feel better about yourself for having let your boss know your thoughts about the situation.*

- *When we are first assertive with a person we have not been assertive with before, they are often shocked because they are not used to it. It may be perceived as aggressiveness if in the past we have been passive in that situation, or it may be seen as being 'soft' if we have been aggressive in the past. Gradually people will get used to our new behaviour and respect us more for it.*

- *We often need to use the 'broken record technique'. That is, to say the same assertive statement several times before it is actually heard. It feels a bit strange at first. For example, if this is the third time in a row you have been asked to stay back on a Friday night you might have to keep on saying, 'I realise unforeseen things come up; however, it is no longer satisfactory for me to have to stay back on a Friday night, especially without warning'.*

- *To come across assertively it is important to be clear about our rights in the situation. Often we have unconstructive self-talk that sabotages our efforts to be assertive.*

Consider now a situation in your life where you feel frustrated, angry or depressed. What do you need to express? Could you use the three steps to assertiveness and the above list of points to start asserting yourself in this situation?

CHALLENGING SELF-LIMITING BELIEFS

Even when we know and practise the skills for being assertive, many of us are afraid of speaking openly and honestly about what we think, feel and need because we have so many self-limiting beliefs. Our thinking is effective when it enables us to feel good about ourselves and behave towards others in ways that work well for them and for us. We commonly think that outer events or situations are directly responsible for our subsequent feelings and behaviour. However, how we respond to a situation will be a result of how we interpret it. And how we interpret it will depend on our inner thinking and self-talk.

There are many self-limiting thoughts that can be responsible for non-assertive behaviour. Thoughts such as, 'I mustn't rock the boat', 'I mustn't let the family down' or, 'I must always do what the boss says', may stop us expressing our true thoughts and feelings. Consider whether you have self-sabotaging thoughts that are stopping you being assertive. In your own words create a substitute thought pattern to assist you to become more assertive by using the following three steps to challenge self-sabotaging thoughts.

Three steps to challenge self-limiting thoughts
- *Step 1*   *Stop and listen to what is going on in your head, so you can identify what you are thinking and saying to yourself.*
- *Step 2*   *Determine whether your thoughts are self-limiting and counterproductive and lead to negative and unhelpful feelings and behaviours.*
- *Step 3*   *If they are, substitute them with other thoughts that you know will work better for you.*

I suggest you now look at three areas of your life where you want to assert yourself. Become aware of any self-limiting thought patterns around these situations and decide from today to challenge them. You will be surprised at how much your world starts to change once you start challenging your thinking and asserting yourself.

Nurturing your Self

When I ask clients how they nurture themselves they often don't know what I mean. Even when I explain that I am asking what they do to take care of themselves they still can't answer because they haven't thought about it before. Often there isn't anything they do for themselves. When we are moving through midlife transition much energy is needed to navigate all the changes, both internally and externally. If we don't nurture our Self, our energy source will become depleted and we may become ill. How do you nurture your Self? For balance and a sense of wellbeing we need to nurture our Self physically, emotionally, intellectually and spiritually. Some activities, such as tai chi or yoga, can nurture us on all four levels, but mostly we need to consciously adopt a variety of attitudes to nurture our Self on all these levels.

For example, we nurture ourself physically by eating the right food. If we do not put the right petrol in our car it eventually does not run as well. In fact one day it might stop completely. It is the same with our body. If we look after our body by giving it what it needs to remain physically healthy, it will reward us by allowing us to move through life with energy and vitality. Do you notice how your body feels after eating different types of food? Have you taken the time to learn about good nutrition?

We nurture ourself by considering carefully what we feed our mind. As much as possible we should fill our mind with healthy thoughts and ideas. During the more turbulent times of mid-life transition we can find great solace by surrounding ourself with well-chosen books, television or radio programs. Listening to peaceful music can also be restful on many levels.

During midlife it is important to exercise, but it needs to be done in a balanced way and to be something we enjoy doing. Walking is easy exercise, although you may prefer jogging, swimming or some other physical activity. At midlife it can be tempting to suddenly start pushing our body physically as a way of deluding our self that our body is not ageing. It is important to choose a balanced approach to exercise with a focus on enjoyment and wellbeing rather than on achieving goals. If we push ourselves to do overstrenuous exercise at midlife it can have drastic results. Remember, a focus at midlife is to create balance!

We nurture ourself when we place around us people who encourage us to pursue our dreams and to keep creating a life that suits the person we are. This does not mean running away from responsibilities. However, relationships may change at midlife as we choose to finally make time for activities that bring joy and passion into our life, and spend our leisure time with people we can share our expanding interests with.

Ensuring you have these self-empowering skills on board at midlife will assist you to negotiate all the inevitable hazards as you navigate the river of your life. Do you have them on board?

CHAPTER 15

integrating Feeling and Thinking

For male executives, a shift in character often means a move in the direction of the 'feminine', embracing a reduction (even if modest) in their investment in work and an increase in their investment in personal relationships. For men to make this shift at midlife is to redefine themselves as being less thoroughly wrapped up in the quest for mastery, power, and rationality and more concerned with cultivating closer, mutual, emotionally expressive relationships.

R. Kaplan, W. Drath & J. Kofodimos, *Beyond Ambition*

PERSONALITY THEORIES ATTEMPT to organise observations of people by providing an underlying framework for classifying and describing behaviour. None of the theories introduced to me while at university seemed to be of much practical use once I started practising as a psychologist. By my mid-thirties I was feeling professionally disillusioned. I had been well trained and clients were satisfied; however, to me there was something missing. As I considered making a career move, I questioned whether I wanted to continue working as a psychologist. After a significant daydream and other synchronistic happenings (which I discuss in Chapter 19), I finally decided to create my own business, consulting to organisations. Just as I made this change it was suggested that it would be useful for me to learn about the Myers-Briggs Type Indicator (MBTI). I remember sitting in the four-day seminar in absolute wonder. After validating my own personality type, so much about myself that had bewildered me throughout my life became clear. Understanding my personality type also affirmed my decision to become a consultant. My personality type indicated that for me, 'life is a creative adventure full of exciting possibilities'. Life as a consultant was much more likely to offer me this than my previous work. At last I had a theory and framework to help me understand myself and others.

I found that psychological type theory as developed by Jung was accessible for an everyday understanding of personality. It helped me to understand and explain normal behavioural variations among 'normal' people. Even though the style and language Jung used to describe his system can be confusing, Katharine Briggs and Isabel Briggs Myers provided an easily understandable interpretation of Jung's original work with their development of the MBTI.

Honouring the Feeling man

As I learnt about and then used the MBTI in my consulting, counselling and coaching, it affirmed for me something I had intuitively felt all my life. Some boys and men quite naturally want to display behaviours that have been traditionally assigned to girls and women, while some girls and women quite naturally want to display behaviours that have been traditionally assigned to boys and men. Today we are more enlightened. Those with sons and daughters, nieces and nephews, and those working with young people, readily perceive this, but in the 1950s and 1960s these observations were only made with unease. The little boy who seemed a bit 'soft' was told he needed to toughen up, while the girl who seemed too forthright was told she needed to develop her gentler qualities.

Were you the sort of boy who found playground fights distasteful, hated conflict of any type and would do anything to avoid it except when you felt another was being treated unfairly? Or did you take up long-distance running because you abhorred the rough and tumble of the footy field? Or, if you did take up a team sport, did you get into trouble from the coach for focusing more on the team than on winning? If so, you might be what I have come to understand through my work with the MBTI as a 'Feeling man'.

As I introduced clients to the MBTI, I would often be witness to a process I thought of as 'honouring the Feeling man'. I'll describe the work I did with George and the team he led to illustrate what I mean.

I was approached by a multinational corporation to introduce the MBTI to one of their Information Technology groups. The focus of the professional development was on individual and team development. After some introductory exercises I explained to the group that although our behaviour seems random, it is not at all. Once we know what to look for we can see that each of us has our own preferred way of doing things. We have a preference for what motivates and energises us; the way we take in information and communicate with others; the way we make decisions; and the way we plan our time and respond to change. An understanding of our own preferences through personality type can enhance our understanding of ourself, our motivations, our natural strengths and our potential areas for growth. It is self-affirming. These understandings encourage us to appreciate people who are different from us. We are born with a certain personality type and how this develops depends on our environment. Some environments will encourage development of our true type, others will discourage it.

I administered the MBTI to George and his team, and then for the rest of the morning I facilitated various exercises to assist them to understand the framework on which the MBTI is based. I demonstrated to them what is meant by 'preference' in the framework by comparing it to our preference for one hand over another when writing. They agreed that they could write with either hand but with their preferred hand it was easier, their writing flowed and they were competent. I explained that similarly, in life, if we know our personality type and thus our preferences and structure our work and personal lives around using these preferences, most of the time our life and the way we go about doing the things within it will seem easy, will flow and we will feel competent.

The MBTI model

I went on to describe the four paired preferences on which the MBTI is based. I explained the first pair are opposite attitudes or orientations of energy—Extraversion (E) or Introversion (I). (In the MBTI 'Extraversion' is spelt with an 'a'.) The next two are opposite mental functions—how we go about gathering information about the world, our perception—Sensing (S) or Intuition (N) and how we reach conclusions about what we have perceived, our judgment—Thinking (T) or Feeling (F). Myers added a fourth pair of opposite attitudes, reflecting our orientation towards the world—Judging (J) or Perceiving (P). People are born with a preference for one of each pair of these opposing tendencies. Therefore, within the MBTI model, with all possible combinations, you get sixteen different personality types.

The first paired preferences—Extraversion (E) and Introversion (I) are about energy flow and focus. If you are an extravert you tend to focus on and be energised by the outer world of people and things. You will therefore tend to become de-energised and tired if you spend too much time by yourself. In contrast, if you are an introvert you tend to focus on and be energised by your inner world of thoughts and reflections. If you are with people for too long you will become de-energised and tired. Remember with all the preferences we are not talking about either/or, we are talking about *preference*, so you will be drawn towards both, but to one more than the other.

The next preference is about how you take in information and perceive the world. Do you rely primarily on your five senses as a means of gathering information and prefer things presented to you in an exact and sequential manner? If so, you have a preference for Sensing (S) and you are very aware of your physical surroundings. Or do you gather information using your five senses then immediately translate it through your intuition, looking for possibilities, meanings and the relationships between and among variables? If so, you prefer Intuition (N) and you have a preference for looking beyond what is actually there. For example, two colleagues are working on a project—one preferring Sensing, the other Intuition. The person preferring Sensing (S) will easily notice the details that need attending to in the project, and only after attending to the details will they be able to focus more on the big picture. The colleague preferring Intuition (N) will focus on the big-picture aspect of the project with ease, and will only then be able to focus on the details.

The third preference is about how you go about making decisions. Do you prefer to make logical decisions—in which case you have a preference for Thinking (T), or do you prefer to make decisions based on what is important to you and/or to others and have a preference for Feeling (F)? Remember, I am only talking about decision-making style here. Although Thinking and Feeling are different processes they often result in the same outcome.

For example, two managers are evaluating a decision about making one of their workers redundant. At first, the Thinking manager focuses on the organisation's needs while the Feeling manager focuses on the needs of the worker. Only after they have used their preferred decision-making function can they then move on to look at other aspects of the process. In fact, if both managers work together, with ease, they will come up with a decision that takes in the needs of the organisation and the needs of the worker, a much better decision than if only one aspect is taken into account. The difference between the two processes is that the Thinking manager is objective and removed while the Feeling manager is totally involved in a subjective evaluation. Both care, think and feel, but the routes by which each arrives at the final conclusion are very different.

The final preference is to do with how we like to structure our outer world. This is the one I can usually tell by looking at a person's desk or bedroom floor. A person who prefers judging (J) likes a structured, well-organised, decisive lifestyle. Their desk will tend to be neat, especially at the end of the day. At night when they take off their clothes they will tend to put them neatly on a chair or hang them up. A perceiver (P) prefers a less decisive lifestyle that goes with the flow. Their desk will usually have piles of documents on it. They usually know where things are and they will only clean up when they are having difficulty locating things. When they take their clothes off they might just step out of them and leave them where they fall or throw them onto a chair. They will perhaps sort them out for the wash or hang them up after several days when they feel things have got out of hand.

To assist you in working out which are your natural preferences I have included a table listing likely characteristics for each preference. You might like to refer to it now.

Table of MBTI preferences

Listed below are characteristics often found in people with that particular preference.

Where do you prefer to focus your attention? From where do you get energy?

Extraversion (E)	Introversion (I)
Focus on the external environment	*Focus on the inner world*
Prefer to communicate through talking	*Prefer to communicate through writing*
Talk things over in order to understand	*Think things through to understand*
Learn best by discussing or doing	*Learn best through reflection*
Broad range of interests	*Few interests, but in depth*
Sociable and expressive	*Private and contained*
Readily take initiative	*Take initiative with the very important*

How do you prefer to deal with information?

Sensing (S)	Intuition (N)
Drawn to present realities	*Drawn to future possibilities*
Focus on what is real and actual	*Focus on patterns and meaning*
Move methodically towards conclusions	*Form quick conclusions— follow hunches*
Understand through practical application	*Understand by clarifying ideas, theories*
Remember details with ease	*Remember details as part of pattern*
Trust experience	*Trust inspiration*
Factual	*Imaginative*

How might others describe you when you make decisions?

Thinking (T)	Feeling (F)
Analytical	*Empathetic*
Use logic to make decisions	*Use personal values to make decisions*
Strive for objective truth	*Strive for harmony*
May be 'tough-minded'	*May be 'tender-hearted'*
Use cause-and-effect thinking	*Guided by personal values*
Reasonable	*Compassionate*
Fair—want people treated equally	*Fair—want people treated as individuals*

How do you prefer to deal with the outer world?

Judging (J)	Perceiving (P)
Organised, systematic, structured	*Flexible, spontaneous, casual*
Decisive	*Like to leave things open to change*
Make short- and long-term plans	*Adapt and change plans with ease*
Avoid last-minute rush	*Energised by last-minute rush*

Note: *Some words used for the MBTI preferences are familiar to us, but their meaning is somewhat different to our everyday use. 'Extravert' does not mean talkative; 'Introvert' does not mean shy; 'Feeling' does not mean emotional; 'Judging' does not mean judgmental; and 'Perceiving' does not mean perceptive.*

GEORGE

In the rest of this chapter I want to focus on the third set of paired preferences, Thinking and Feeling, and to do this I will tell you more about the work I did with George. When I explained the differences between a person who preferred Thinking (T) to a person who preferred Feeling (F), George showed keen interest. I also noted that he was the only one in his team who had a preference for F. Over lunch George told me how different he had felt all his life. He remembered getting teased at kindergarten when he showed his feelings when playing with other boys. In his family and at an all-boys' school, he eventually found ways to hide his differences. Later on he discovered that he loved being around certain girls. Their conversations always sounded interesting to him. Once he started having girlfriends it made a huge difference. He explained he had always structured his work to have time with his wife, children and friends. This intimate contact was essential for his wellbeing.

He had worked in the company for twenty years. As he had risen through management he had often felt at odds with the way decisions were made. While others were focusing on how to get the job done most expediently, or how to reach targets, he was focused on the welfare of individuals and teams. At first he would go along with the general opinion; however, with increasing confidence he started to speak his mind. Since his mid-thirties he has increasingly felt a need to find ways to openly express at work what he calls his 'soft side'. Now he knows he is recognised as a man who is good at dealing with 'people issues' and that he has an intuitive understanding of how to deal with others in a way that many of those around him don't.

When Isabel Briggs Myers did her research on the MBTI in 1957 she found that almost 40 per cent of men had a preference for Feeling and that almost 40 per cent of women had a preference for Thinking. That was over 40 years ago yet people still talk about personality and behavioural differences between men and women, instead of differences that are more related to differences in personality. Once people learn about personality type, they don't do that anymore and Feeling men and Thinking women stop wondering what is wrong with them.

Over the past fifteen years a variety of men at midlife have consulted me for career change management counselling. I have administered the MBTI with nearly all of them and many of them indicated a preference for Feeling. I now wonder whether Feeling men of the baby boomer generation are more likely to experience a strong need to make career changes at midlife than those who have a preference for Thinking. Especially as many of them have worked in a traditional male thinking culture in the first half of life.

Despite this career challenge faced by many Feeling men at midlife, they in many ways have an easier task at midlife than Thinking men. They have a disposition that supports the development of their feeling life and their feminine side—two aspects essential to develop for midlife transition.

THINKING MEN CAN BE
PEOPLE-FOCUSED TOO

I am not suggesting that men who have a preference for T will not be able to display people-focused attitudes in their work or family life. It's just that it won't come to them as naturally as it does for the F man, and at midlife a T man will usually have to do much work to balance out his T and F.

Life was often easier for a T boy. He fitted into the stereotypical expectations of how a young boy should be. His ability to be detached, objective and logical made it easy for him to groom himself for a man's world. You wouldn't have to look far to find him in the offices of a large, bureaucratic organisation. A culture with a focus on task, tough-mindedness, analytical process, mastery and problem-solving is a comfortable environment for him and is rewarded with generous salary increases and promotion. However, if he is unable to develop the behaviours and attitudes of his less preferred F, difficulties will arise in his personal and professional life, especially at midlife.

In the first half of life, T men often have allowed the women in their life to carry their feeling for them. As a consequence they have repressed an important part of themselves that is essential for their full growth and wholeness. At the same time many women at midlife move beyond the socially sanctioned role of carrying a man's feeling world. They come to a stage where they refuse to mother, refuse to live with men who are emotionally unavailable, refuse to manage the relationship aspect of a man's life. As there is withdrawal of this support a man will suffer the loss of her emotional and psychological energy, and can feel overwhelmed by unmet dependency needs. To explain to you how a man might start developing his less preferred Feeling I'll tell you about the work I did with Paul.

PAUL

Paul, a senior manager in a large multinational corporation, came to me for coaching. I had introduced a performance management system into his workplace a couple of years earlier. We had spent some time together and when Paul sensed he was getting into difficulties he decided to come and have a chat.

He recently got results from a feedback process implemented throughout his section, whereby those he worked with gave him feedback anonymously on various aspects of his managerial style. He was troubled to find that several of those working under him perceived him as not a good listener and as having little time for them. Two members of his team had recently handed in their resignations, citing difficulties in working with him as one of their reasons for leaving. His boss had called him into his office, thrown onto his desk the results of this feedback, and told him to do something about it. Paul was devastated.

At the same time his thirteen-year-old son was in trouble at school for smoking dope and his wife was complaining that he always seemed preoccupied with work. The only bright part of his life was time with his fifteen-year-old daughter. He felt everything was piling up on him. When his boss called him in 'to have a chat' Paul appeared to take it calmly, as was his way; however, on the way home he got a huge shock when he suddenly burst into tears. He decided it was time to come to see me.

Over several sessions it became clear that with Paul's focus on results and getting the job done, many if not all of the people-focus of his life was being neglected, including focus on his own needs. He had been sleeping poorly for a couple of years, often tossing and turning, thinking about all that needed to be done. His boss kept on putting the pressure on him to get even better results and so he felt he always had to be pushing those he managed to achieve these results. He explained it as like being in a pressure cooker. He felt tense, stiff in the body, and often the only time he felt relaxed was after swimming or after he and his wife 'made love'.

The behaviours and attitudes that go with the T preference are so prevalent in senior management that it is often assumed that the behaviours of being tough-minded, having task focus and using logic are synonymous with being effective. In an effort to remain focused on the task Paul avoided behaviours that seemed to take up too much time. Paul admitted he avoided people-related issues, especially when emotions were involved, because he never knew quite what to do. Recently there had been conflict between two of his team members. He had been asked to step in but instead had just told them to 'get on with the job'.

After going over Paul's management style feedback with him, asking him about his work and family life, and also completing the MBTI and going through his personal strengths and weaknesses, I suggested to Paul that I spend six months supporting him through some fairly intensive personal development. Most of it would be done 'on the job', so to speak. I would set him some areas to focus on for development, we would do some role-playing where necessary, and then he would try out some new behaviours. He could keep regular contact through the telephone and email and we would meet face-to-face fortnightly. I emphasised that without changing some of his attitudes, the changed behaviours would be seen as false. Below you will find some of the things Paul and I worked on over a period of six months. Could you benefit from involving yourself in a process similar to this?

Commitment to the process

I emphasised to Paul that if he wanted to make changes it would involve a commitment to a potentially painful process of self-examination and of getting in touch with his emotional vulnerability. There needed to be a commitment of emotional energy, courage to make changes and, most importantly, commitment of time. The primary way to develop his Feeling function was in relationships. There were three relationships Paul wanted to focus on. The first was with his colleagues, the second with his wife and the final one was with his son. I added two others: the relationship with himself, and the challenge of finding a man with whom he would endeavour to develop a more 'feeling-based' relationship. This final suggestion of mine was still on the 'back burner' as we completed our six months of coaching, although I discussed my suggestions with Paul so he could use them down the track if he chose to.

Listening to colleagues

As with many men who have a preference for T, Paul was not an effective listener. Feedback suggested that Paul's colleagues rarely felt he listened to them, even when they made a time to see him in his office. These are some of the suggestions I gave to him. First, I emphasised to Paul that to truly listen to another he needed to give the other person his full attention. This means diverting the phone; putting away anything that might distract him, such as a report he was working on; to have eye contact, but not stare; and to convey with his body language that the conversation was the most important thing in his life right now. Second, I encouraged him to turn off his logical self, suspend judgment and just listen. Third, to strive to understand how the other person was feeling and thinking by looking for clues from their body language. I also suggested he should ask some clarifying questions, but not too many as it could sound like an inquisition, and use minimal encouragers such as nodding his head or just saying 'u-ha'. At first Paul felt daunted by all these suggestions so we did some role-playing. I also explained that although some of these new behaviours may feel strange at first, this was only because they were new to him. With practice they would come to him with some ease—a bit like learning to drive a car.

Relationship with his wife

I encouraged Paul to set aside time each week that he dedicated as time with his wife. I suggested they should vary how they spent this time. I encouraged him to practise the same effective listening skills I had outlined for him to use at work. I also encouraged him to talk about himself; to share something he was vulnerable about, perhaps especially some of the things he had shared with me. Paul said that his wife was not interested in sex. He admitted that neither was he. I suggested they spend fifteen minutes just holding each other and then talk about how this felt. I also suggested they think of things they enjoy doing together and to make time for these, as well as encouraging each other to pursue their own interests.

Relationship with his son

I encouraged Paul to consciously bring a Feeling component into how he related to his son. An important part of that was for Paul to feel comfortable sharing some of his feelings with his son. He also had to be ready for that 'golden moment' when his son wanted to share with him. I encouraged Paul not to have any expectations, that it would take time. Paul admitted that his responsiveness with his son was more emotionally blunted than it was with his daughter. He decided to talk with his son about what they could enjoy doing together.

Time with self

I emphasised to Paul that this was actually his most important relationship. Until he learnt to make time for himself, listen to his own inner feelings, thoughts and desires, he would not be able to do this with ease with another. First, I suggested he make at least fifteen minutes a day available, either just sitting or using a simple relaxation technique to quieten his mind. He should also notice any feelings that came up. Second, I encouraged him to remember his dreams; to keep a book and a pen beside his bed so that on waking he could write down anything he remembered, especially how he felt in the dream. Third, I suggested that at the end of the day, before going to sleep, he review his day, remembering how he felt at different times of the day. Finally, I asked him to, at the beginning of every day, consider what he could put in his day, no matter how small, to make it more enjoyable for him.

Time with a male friend

At the time I realised my suggestion of a feeling-based relationship with another male was a big request of Paul; however, I wanted to plant the idea. Knowing men don't easily share their feelings with other men, and knowing this is even more difficult for men who have a T preference, I nevertheless gave Paul some suggestions he might like to implement at a later date. I asked him to consider whether he knew a man he could ask to spend time with and share stories. He acknowledged he had been conditioned to not have this sort of relationship with other men. We talked about the feelings that came up for him even at the suggestion. I also encouraged him to consider hugging the husband goodbye as well as the wife when out with his wife and other couples.

USING BOTH FEELING AND THINKING
CREATES BALANCE

To rely mainly on just Thinking or Feeling deprives us of a richness and creativity that can only come by bringing both into our way of being. At midlife, our psyche encourages us to create balance in all aspects of our life. In MBTI terms this means a focus on the development of our less preferred side. For a man with a preference for F this will mean the development of his T tendencies. Given the conditioning he is likely to have received because he is male, an F man often arrives at midlife balanced in his ability to use both F and T attitudes and behaviours with the people and situations in his life. In contrast, a man with a preference for Thinking, such as Paul, will often arrive at midlife with much personal work to do to create balance as he has inhabited a world that has reinforced his preference. As a T man starts to develop his F side at midlife, it may at first feel bewildering and cumbersome. But with a personal commitment he can develop the capacity for an easy interplay between the two. For an F man, who has been conditioned to suppress much of his natural, softer side in the first half of life, the acknowledgment of his F side at midlife seems like the honouring of an old friend that has at last been allowed to come home.

CHAPTER 16

sex and intimacy

There is a major shift in what they [men] value in a relationship
as they enter Second Adulthood and later stages. The need for
intimacy and companionship eclipses the importance of sex.

Gail Sheehy, *New Passages*

THE MEN I INTERVIEWED talked about their sex lives. As I wasn't
asking any leading questions, they always initiated these conversations. They talked in a variety of ways about sex. Many said it had
been a significant focus of their attention since puberty; others
talked about how they found themselves distracted by it; a couple
talked about difficulties with intimacy; and some discussed the
challenge and the joy of bringing more intimacy into their sex lives.

SEXUALITY AT MIDLIFE

Bill, in his early forties, mentioned how he noticed himself fantasising about being with other women, but never actually followed up
on these fantasies. In the past couple of years he realised he fantasised
most when things weren't going well in his life. He had decided his
fantasies were a way of avoiding looking at these issues. Elias, in
his early fifties, talked about how all through his married life he had
had affairs. He explained to me how this pattern had started very

early on in his marriage. Before marriage one of his girlfriends had openly been with another man while they were together—her rationale being that it was okay because she wasn't emotionally involved with the other man. Elias accepted this with her and then carried this approach into his marriage. He had many affairs over the years but because he hadn't developed an emotional attachment he thought it didn't count. His wife did not know about these liaisons.

Other men, in their late forties and early fifties, talked about how their sexual desire had changed. It was still an important part of their life but it was as though the energy around the whole experience had changed. They found their lovemaking was now less focused on orgasm and more on touching. It was gentler. One talked about how it was not as easy to get an erection, nevertheless he and his wife had found different ways of loving and in many ways he felt more satisfied. He thought she was too. Below are the stories of two of the men I interviewed. These men's stories affirm that each of us is able to find our own unique way to transform our relationship to our sexuality at midlife.

Ross (46 years)

I met Jill in my late twenties and we married within a year. All seemed fine for several years, but after our first child was born our sex life tapered off significantly. I found this really hard. I felt rejected. When I look back I feel pretty appalled about some of my behaviour around that time. I remember almost pleading with her. I'd never force myself on her though.

At my work there is this older guy, Brian, who in many ways has been a mentor for me over the years. I discuss all sorts of work matters with him. I somehow found I was talking to him about what was happening at home. I was feeling pretty desperate. The night before while in bed Jill had exploded at me saying, 'Stop putting on those little boy voices. Why can't you act like a man?' I told him about it and in talking it over he got me to see that I needed to change my attitude and behaviour. After our discussion that day, I created a sort of mantra that I would say to myself. It went something like this: 'I will never whine again. If I feel like sex I will say it straight out and if Jill says no, I'll just turn over, no matter how difficult it is.' And I was able to do this and by changing my behaviour it shifted so much between us. It was a turning point. It was as though once I just expressed openly where I was at, without having any expectations around the outcome, the more I got what I wanted. Everything between us became so less intense, both in and out of the bedroom. We started laughing and talking in bed and experiencing a whole lot more variety in our sex life.

I'm not saying it has all been plain sailing since then. It certainly hasn't. Sometimes sex can still be an issue between us but now I realise it is often to do with my attitude, or hers, around a variety of other aspects either within ourselves or within our relationship. To become more aware of ourselves and of what was happening between us, we both separately had some counselling. Some of the things I have come to understand are:

• Sexual intercourse that is not equally enjoyed by your partner is barren and, if that state continues, downright depressing.
• Conversely, reaching a state where your partner initiates sex and enjoys it, and you can see your attitude helps her to really enjoy it, is one of the most deeply fulfilling and satisfying feelings. In a long-term relationship this doesn't happen all the time. It is a shifting sand and, when missing for a while, presents the challenge to both partners to reclaim it.
• A real breakthrough is to achieve a relationship where both partners can laugh during intercourse and not be too intense about it all. However, you can only be light-hearted if you feel secure in yourself.
• It is vital to establish a relationship where your partner can let you know, in a non-threatening way, exactly what he or she needs to get maximum pleasure. Again, you can reach that intimacy and then lose it—then reclaim it and so on.

Now, ten years later, I realise how much that initial conversation with Brian led to a series of changes in how I experience sex and how much more my wife and I talk and share what's going on inside us, both in the bedroom and in our daily lives. I suppose that is intimacy.

Jack

I became very interested in getting to know parts of myself as part of my spiritual journey. In my mid-thirties I acknowledged I had these desires that I didn't seem to have total control of. I was determined that I would win this battle over them. I used all my willpower to control my desire for sex. It worked for a few months but I became quite ill. So then over a period of fifteen years I went on a quest to understand my sexuality. Very quickly I realised I couldn't fight it and I also couldn't see an easy way to transform it.

My wife and I were clear that our sexual needs were very different. She was also clear that she wasn't prepared to make too many compromises. She was accepting that my needs were different to hers and that there was nothing wrong with mine. She just wasn't prepared to satisfy them to my level. I think she would have been happy for us to maybe sleep with each other once a fortnight or once a month. And my preference was a bit more than that. Not that I wanted it every day but maybe once or twice a week was something I think I could have settled for. Not that I did anything unreasonable. If she didn't want sex, I never forced her, never pushed her. But it was quite obvious that my mood was affected and I did not like that. And so that started me on my journey really, to try to understand that part of myself. I wanted to change my relationship with my sexuality so as to get more control over it.

I meditated a lot, I observed myself and I talked to one male friend in particular about it. And I wrote about it very intensely in my journal. Then I just started to explore this whole business of sexuality and the passions, the needs and the desires. It became a huge focus for me and I just wanted to get to the bottom of it.

It was a much longer journey than I thought it would be. And at some stage I felt I needed to experiment. With my wife's approval I visited regularly, for two or three years, prostitutes and sex shops to explore parts of my sexuality. And so I sort of made a study of it. I would go into a sex shop and just look at all the different magazines and all the different things and I would just observe myself, what really got my attention. Afterwards I gave myself permission to experiment with what had caught my fancy, being very conscious about safety aspects.

I came to a point where I think I had experienced all the things that caught my fancy in the sex shops. I had ticked off everything. And there was still this desire there. The desire still hadn't been satisfied and I came to a point, in my early forties, when I realised that nobody in the world, not even the most perfect woman, would be able to satisfy my longings. I cried for days. That was a huge insight for me because what it indicated to me—what it really shouted to me—was that this focus since puberty on sexuality and women was actually an illusion. It just wasn't possible for these desires to be permanently satisfied. I realised that the more I tried to satisfy the illusion, the stronger it grew in me. And that was very painful because it also indicated that all I had been doing and all these longings were just to cover up my fear of not being loved, which I then traced back to how my mother related to me. She wasn't a physical person at all. She never gave me cuddles. With this insight I was able to transform part of these longings, and eventually I developed a friendship with that part of myself.

Insights on sex and intimacy

As the men I interviewed talked spontaneously about their sexuality, it was clearly an important subject for men at midlife. But how was

I, a woman, to write about it? I didn't feel comfortable as a woman discussing this subject with much authority, although through understandings I had come to in my research on midlife I had developed my own ideas. So in writing this chapter I am not wanting to suggest that I am an expert on sexuality. There are many practitioners who specialise in this area and if you have some ongoing sexual issues I recommend you consult one of them. In this chapter I will refer to some of the books I have read and then bring in some of my own ideas. I hope that some of the suggestions assist you in deepening your understanding of how to bring balance into the way you experience and express your sexuality, if this is something you believe you need to do.

While I was pondering about the content of this chapter, I visited one of the large bookshops in my home city, Melbourne. I walked over to the men's section, picked up a book titled, *Male Lust: Pleasure, Power and Transformation*, and immediately opened it up at an essay by Steve Bearman called 'Why Men Are So Obsessed With Sex'. I agreed with many of the points Bearman made in his essay, and I asked several men to read it. Some of them at first had reservations about it; however, once they gave it further thought they agreed that much of Bearman's discussion fitted in with their own experiences around sex and intimacy. I also believe that much of Bearman's discussion can fit into aspects of a woman's journey around sex and intimacy. While writing this chapter there are a couple of other books I have found very informative, thought-provoking and useful— *Passionate Marriage* by David Schnark, and *New Passages* and *Passages for Men,* both by Gail Sheehy.

INTIMACY AND MEN AT MIDLIFE

In her book, *New Passages,* Gail Sheehy reports on her research findings that the highly educated, professional men she surveyed noticed a major shift in what they valued from their intimate partner once they passed their mid-forties. Although feeling less secure in their sexual prowess, their need for intimacy and companionship eclipsed the importance of sex. Sheehy explains:

> What they mean by intimacy is closeness, emotional warmth, tenderness, private jokes, and a mutual acceptance of vulnerabilities. A new chemistry seems to come out of this admission of their need for closeness that binds their feelings into a more subtle sexual passion. (p. 327)

In *Passionate Marriage,* David Schnark uses the concept of differentiation to explore what is necessary to experience intimacy. He explains differentiation as, 'the process by which we become more uniquely ourselves by maintaining ourselves in relationship with those we love' (p. 51). He goes on to say, 'When you've achieved a high level of differentiation . . . you're more capable of expressing who you are in the face of neutral or even negative responses from your partner' (p. 107).

Schnark's concept of differentiation is similar to Jung's concept of individuation. Both terms are referring to a journey of wholeness that leads to increasingly knowing, being and affirming your Self. A way of picturing the interplay between differentiation or individuation and intimacy is that the greater differentiated or individuated you are the more able you are to hold on to your Self in a relationship. The more differentiated or individuated we are, the more we know and trust our Self. This makes it more possible for us to share our Self. It can also be assumed that the more sure we feel within our Self, the more risks we will be willing to take in sharing all parts of our Self with our partner, including our vulnerabilities.

From my experience, I can feel quite clear and confident within myself while not in a relationship, and then when in a relationship have the tendency to lose my sense of Self. As I increasingly individuate I am getting better at holding onto my Self in relationships; however, it is an ongoing struggle for me. I am gradually developing my ability to remain differentiated while in relationships. This for me is one of the many benefits of an intimate relationship. If I am willing to be present to and share my vulnerability and concerns within the relationship it leads to greater Self understanding and increasing intimacy. Schnark also argues that any difficulties in our sex life will be a mirror of our relationship as a whole. He suggests that by working on the issues in our bedroom, we will at the same time work on the issues outside the bedroom—and vice versa.

> No lovemaking technique can substitute for the erotic charge
> that flows when lovers approach each other with engaging,
> receptive eyes, and the simple trust of being unguarded and
> vulnerable together.

MEN, POTENCY AND MIDLIFE

At midlife a man's psyche is encouraging him to connect with his own inner feminine. Some men continue to pursue the outer feminine rather than do the work to connect with their own and this is typically seen in a man who continues to re-partner with younger and younger women. Rather than connecting with his own inner feminine he finds it in another. In contrast, if a man does the work to connect with his inner feminine, feeling world he connects with an aspect of himself that then allows him to have deeper connections with others, especially his intimate partner. For we are only able to connect to another's feeling world to the extent we are able to connect with our own. This type of connection is vital if we are to be able to sustain intimate relationships.

From all that is written about men with potency problems, could it be that difficulties around potency for men at midlife are a reflection of this transformation in the expression of their sexuality? As in every other aspect of his life, a midlife man's psyche is encouraging him to rebalance his relationship with his own sexuality. For example, if he has tended to use a masculine attitude of strength, potency and virility with a focus on performance to express his sexuality in the first half of life, he may easily feel bewildered and even terrified as his psyche encourages him to express his sexuality from a more feminine, feeling attitude. As his sexuality becomes more an expression of connection rather than one of physical prowess, what creates arousal for him will start to change. If he doesn't understand the transformation that is taking place within him, he may cling on to his old ways of arousal, possibly leading to potency problems. Then, imagining it is a physical problem he may seek out medication. It may be important for him to have a physical check-up to ensure there is nothing physically wrong. However, if he is at midlife, it is also important for him to remind himself that he is at a stage in life where his way of relating to his sexuality is changing. If he doesn't realise what is happening to him, he may look for more and more stimulation from the physical world, such as pornography, to stimulate his arousal. He continues to look to his outer world rather than realising it is in his inner feeling world he will find the link to a new type of arousal for his sexuality. In contrast, if a man at midlife works on connecting with his own feeling world and that of his partner's, this growing intimacy will provide a new type of fuel for arousal in his sex life. In Schnark's words:

> Aging is not the inevitable downward spiral you have learned
> to expect with dread. Many aspects of your feelings and
> thoughts can more than offset declining hormonal drive and
> reflexive responses if you're willing to grow up sexually. (p. 90)

In his essay 'Why Men Are So Obsessed with Sex', Bearman points out that men 'are born sensual creatures with an unlimited capacity to feel and an effortless propensity to deeply connect with all human beings'. He goes on to say that through conditioning they are then encouraged to repress their sensuality, numb their feelings, ignore their bodies, and separate from a natural need for closeness. Young men are then handed sex as the one way to express and experience these very human needs. Sex can quickly become addictive as this becomes the only way men can get relief from the pain of being split off from these important parts of themselves. Bearman explains that sex will only give men temporary relief from these inner needs, and they will then just want more of it as they see this as the only way to get these needs met. He emphasises that he is not denying that sexuality is a 'potent source of love, pleasure, intimacy, sensuality and beauty'. However, in no way can sex fulfil all these needs, and if a man is not to become preoccupied with sex he needs to find ways to break down his conditioning. Bearman encourages men to focus on three areas. First, a man needs to develop his skills to become intimate with himself and others. To do this he will have to develop his feeling world, learning how to go within to understand what he is feeling inside. He will then be able to use this same understanding for those around him. Second, he needs to find ways to bring passion, other than through sex, into his life. Finally, Bearman suggests a man needs to reclaim his body.

RECLAIMING INTIMACY

During the first half of life a man has often focused all his needs for intimate relating and closeness on to his primary relationship. It is she who has helped him to understand his emotional world and even at times articulated it for him. At midlife a man needs to develop the language and skills to understand his own feeling world, for to be intimate with another, we first need to be intimate with ourself. Without doing this inner work, none of us—men or women—can truly relate to another. Instead of thinking in terms of, 'I'm fine', a man needs to take the time to really know those feelings inside him. Some of the men I interviewed did this 'reclaiming' through counselling, others through group work, and a few through developing a life-changing, intimate, non-sexual relationship with another man.

Developing this intimate, non-sexual relationship with another can be a very scary place to go at first and the most important aspect is for a man to feel safe. If he can develop intimacy skills so that he can direct the unconditional love he formerly reserved for people he was sexually attracted to, outward to all kinds of people in all kinds of relationships, he will then be able to get his intimacy needs met in a variety of ways beyond a sexual encounter. As his intimacy needs begin to be fulfilled through a variety of relationships, his relationship with his primary partner will be freed up as he realises that no one person can meet all his needs for closeness. For it is part of our human nature to desire closeness with many people—a closeness that rarely has anything to do with sex.

Ask yourself now:

• How well do you connect to your feeling world?
• How well do you connect to the feeling world of others?
• Do you have an intimate non-sexual relationship with another person? Would you like one?

Reclaiming passion

In her book, *New Passages*, Gail Sheehy states that those men who are open to new experiences at midlife have the highest wellbeing:

When men begin to enjoy cooking or landscaping their homes, or take up musical instruments they once loved, or start studying languages or exploring spiritual or philosophic realms, it is obvious that a major reorganisation of their personalities is in progress. Instead of fighting a transition that allows them to be more, these men are tapping into new sources of energy and pleasure that are available to them naturally. (p. 326)

To open yourself up more to your feeling world, you need to explore the world to find out what can bring the passionate intensity into your life that has previously been reserved for sexual encounters. Ask yourself:

- What besides sex brings passion into my life?
- What dreams and desires could I give birth to or rekindle to bring more vibrancy into my everyday life?
- Where can I feel free to explore and express emotions such as sadness, joy, wonder, anger?

All these feelings are part of all of us, and as we find safe and appropriate ways to express them our being becomes more alive.

RECLAIMING YOUR BODY

Our conditioning in Western culture has encouraged us to become cut off from the sensations of our body. We dwell so much in our minds, rather than in our sensual and feeling worlds that for many it is quite a journey to move energy down through the body. The wearing of a tie to work can even be viewed as an unconscious, symbolic gesture to remind a man that he needs to cut himself off from his body and his feeling world as he goes about his business. What could you do to open yourself up more to the sensations of your body? Would you consider bringing more sensuality into your life by walking barefoot on wet grass, dancing around a room, swimming in the ocean and really feeling the water caressing your body, or taking a massage?

BALANCE IN SEX AND INTIMACY AT MIDLIFE

As with other aspects of his life, a man's psyche is encouraging him to create balance in the way he expresses and experiences his sexuality at midlife. If a man at midlife finds other ways, besides sex, to bring intimate encounters, feelings and sensuality into his life, he can open up to a way of being that he never imagined possible. He can develop a life vibrant with passion, and with closeness to fellow human beings everywhere he goes. In the process his experience of sex and intimacy will be transformed. As Bearman says:

> When sexual desire is purged of desperation, urgency, loneliness and fear, then sex can be inspired by joy and sexual relationships can be healthy and whole. Sex can be an exquisite celebration of intimacy and expression of love, a place for healing, a time to play with all the vigour and enthusiasm we had as children. Sex can be a place to express the passion cultivated by living a vibrant life and to delight in the ecstasy we all deserve. (p. 222)

CHAPTER 17

you are called to your vocation at midlife

*The transitions of life's second half offers a special kind of
opportunity to break with the social conditioning and do
something really new and different.*

William Bridges, *Managing Transitions*

THERE IS A HUGE difference between a job and a vocation. A job
is what we do to earn money to meet the demands of such things as
supporting a partner, ourself, our children, financing our or another's
education and so on. A vocation, derived from the Latin word
vocatus which means 'calling', is what we are called to do. We are all
born with the attributes to fulfil our own particular destiny. This
destiny becomes clear as we become more complete in ourselves.
Our destiny is the contribution we give back to society. It is part of
our individuation to feel that we are productive in society, and so not
responding to our calling will diminish our experience of our Self.
So, any time from our mid-thirties onward we are looking for work
that not only pays the bills but also gives us voice to express our
wholeness, the unique human being we are. Here are some examples
of men who have taken this step at midlife.

Simon, 50, had read and thought about some of the social issues confronting our society like Aboriginal reconciliation, refugees, youth homelessness and drug abuse. He gave support by giving money to the main charities, but always felt it was somewhat indirect and unsatisfactory personally. He explained to me that giving money seemed an anonymous transaction. In his late forties he had felt an urge to contribute more of himself, his time and his talents directly. An opportunity arose when the business he was co-owner of was sold. He had time to spare. Instead of jumping back into full-time business ventures, he looked around and among other things, went to a meeting where he heard an Aboriginal leader speak passionately and eloquently about the causes and the nature of Aboriginal people's problems. He explained how he had built a partnership between his people and corporate and philanthropic leaders, and they were on a journey led by Aboriginal elders to make positive changes in their own society, particularly in the area of creating a real business economy. Simon offered his time, business expertise and contacts and became involved through the local Aboriginal organisations in several areas, ranging from programs that create and operate business enterprises that employ indigenous children (at risk from petrol sniffing, alcohol abuse, theft, suicide) to helping families set up their own small tourism businesses.

Simon told me, 'The places I work in are light years away from the economic, educational, health and social environment of my own comfortable white middle-class urban world so it has been a challenging experience. However, this difference is what has made it a valuable and interesting learning experience for me. In addition I get the bonus of developing friendships with some very fine people.'

Georgio, 40 and single, has been in IT all his life. He worked his way up in the company ever since leaving school at seventeen. Recently, when the company was downsizing and redundancies were being offered, he realised how sick of his job he was. He took the redundancy package and for the past year has travelled and is now halfway through a cooking course. He had ideas of becoming a chef;

however, now that he has looked into it he realises a chef's life is too pressured for him. He wants to find a way of earning a living which allows him to lead a more balanced life. He is also realising how lonely he feels.

He would like a girlfriend, yet says he feels shy with women. On further questioning this doesn't appear to be so. He easily talks to women. His perception that he is shy appears to be inner talk he has carried over from when young. When I point out the incongruence between his description of his relaxed talks with women in his local bushwalking club and his self-talk about 'being shy with women' he expresses surprise. We discuss how he might meet women who suit him. He does meet women through various clubs he is a member of, although by our third interview he has also joined a 'matchmaking service'. It is one that I have recommended and that I know is reputable.

Georgio is now considering eventually opening up a café. In the meantime he plans to get work experience through some salaried work. He recognises he has much to learn about managing a food business before he ventures out on his own. He also wants to make sure he leaves enough time to pursue his personal goal of bringing some intimacy into his life.

Vince, 41, did an apprenticeship in his dad's plumbing business straight out of school. He said that through all this time he was happy in the work. When young he had thought of going into teaching, but, when his dad was so keen for him to join the business he changed his mind. In his mid-thirties he started running a local Scout group and this reawakened his interest in teaching. In his late-thirties he started to train as a teacher.

I had a deep sense that it was right for me. Financial consider-ations didn't come into it. My income was more than halved but I had a sense of what was really important to me and this was much more significant. My partner, Robert, earns a good income. We won't have the expensive holidays we had in the past. Sure we don't have as much money; however, I am deeply contented and we have more time together.

Chris, 45, has had a successful career in advertising but for the past three years has increasingly realised how much he detests many aspects of his work. However, he feels locked in. Married with two children at private schools, a large home in the inner city, and a holiday house, he explains that all of this takes a lot of looking after. He can't see a way out. Recently he has been feeling very tense and is having out-of-character angry outbursts, especially at his son. He's also drinking at night—a habit he only started four years ago.

When I asked Chris whether he could imagine doing anything else, he first replied, 'I don't have a clue'. He said he had spent so many years focused on his work he sometimes felt that this was all he was. By the third counselling session Chris mentioned that while walking in the local park early one morning he had remembered his dreams to become an interior designer.

Thoughts of this former dream now kept on popping into his mind at the oddest moments. He didn't see how he could possibly go and retrain. When I questioned him about his assets he was willing to discuss them with me, although he was still not ready to confront what it might mean materially for his family were he to follow his dreams.

Robert, aged 47 years, works for a large city legal firm. His dad was a lawyer and it had always been assumed in the family that he too would practise law. He enjoyed the law but in his mid-thirties acknowledged he felt there was little if no personal meaning in the work he was doing. He started to reconnect with a yearning to be involved in work that had a social justice focus. And then his firm decided to create three new legal positions. The total focus of these positions would be on non-chargeable legal advice for the not-for-profit sector. Since taking up one of these positions he has never felt so professionally fulfilled.

DISSATISFACTION WITH WORK
AT MIDLIFE IS NORMAL

A job chosen in one's twenties rarely continues to satisfy at midlife. In the first half of life we tend to choose a career with a focus on parental expectations, our own strengths and abilities, potential income—all leading to creating security to meet the expectations of building a secure life structure. This is important work in the first half of life.

It is common to experience feelings of dissatisfaction, alienation and emptiness in work at midlife. This might be expressed by feelings that we have picked the wrong occupation accompanied by feelings of desperation to find the right one before it is too late. Or that the job that has been satisfying for many years now has lost much of its meaning. Or even if work is still meaningful, we have a yearning to express a deeper part of ourselves.

In *The Seven Habits of Highly Effective People* Stephen Covey talks about how we can be so busy climbing up the ladder that we don't notice it is leaning against the wrong wall. I don't believe there is ever truly a 'wrong wall', because no matter what we have done in the past we will have developed skills, had life experiences and learnt things about ourself that we otherwise would not have. So, although at midlife we might feel that we have been in the wrong place all along, this is not so—it just feels that way. It's just that now our psyche is telling us it is time for a change. Don't have regrets about where you have been. Know that much of what you have learnt and developed within yourself will help you in creating your desired future. Also see it as a sign to ensure you make conscious choices about how you develop your working life from here on. Expressing these choices through your work enables you to reflect your growing understanding of who you are.

When a man starts his first job in his teens or early twenties he knows a limited amount about himself. Often, baby boomer men chose careers to fulfil parents' ambitions, rather than their own. Or a career was chosen because a boy was good at certain subjects at school and so there was an automatic conclusion such as, 'You are bright and good at sciences. You should do medicine' or, 'You are good with your hands. Why not join dad and become an electrician?' By the time a man is navigating towards the second half of life he is looking for more personally meaningful reasons about how he will make a living. Thoughts and feelings are bubbling up from deep inside. As he feels a need to express an increasing understanding of his whole self in his work, his psyche is navigating him towards a vocation.

It's not as if you wake up one morning realising you no longer find your present job meaningful and within a week have found your vocation. Nor is it something you can set goals for. A vocation unfolds over several stages, where there is a gradual balancing between the material needs and a need for personal meaning. Around this time, after working full bore, a man also needs to find time to rebalance, give time to his inner world and connect with forgotten dreams. Just as it takes many years to navigate midlife transition, finding your vocation is often a slow unfolding as you become clearer about who you are and what is most important to you. Finding your vocation is seldom a straight path. It's often not until your fifties that you can look back and see why you were drawn to make the choices you did during midlife. Whether you create new opportunities for self-fulfilment in your old job, explore a new way of earning a living, or create more opportunities for personal fulfilment outside your salaried work, you will be drawn to make changes that move you towards your destiny.

I am not suggesting that we all need to change jobs, or even have a salaried job, to find our vocation at midlife. There is no single right way to navigate ourselves towards our vocation. However, once we find our vocation we will see that all our experiences have contributed to our being able to undertake what we are now called to do. Some may find that it is not in their job that they express their vocation. Work is how they earn their living. Outside work is where they fulfil their calling. So our vocation may have nothing to do with earning money. A man may be called to mentor young men in his local community. Or he may be called to be an artist in a time which does not reward art monetarily. For some men, what has been missing in the first half of life is ambition and so at midlife they are drawn to a deeper dedication to work and achievement. But for the vast majority of men the first half of life is a time of over identifying with earning money and achievement and so the second half of life is often a time when the focus is more on personal meaning.

Your inner voice calls you

To find your vocation you have to open up your mind to many possibilities, be patient, look for signs, look for where your energy is drawn, and listen to your inner voice. You have to listen to your inner voice very carefully for often this voice is just a whisper, especially at first. There are also other voices which are your inner saboteurs. Messages you were sent when young, such as, 'You mustn't be selfish. You must be realistic. You can't write. You're no good with people', can stop you from believing it is possible to move towards your dreams. Other societal messages such as, 'You have family responsibilities. You have to save for retirement', also hinder you as you look at what changes are possible. Certainly you need to remain responsible to your commitments; however, from my interviews, even men who have substantial assets will say they still need to work long hours and earn a large amount of money, rather than make available some time to pursue their dreams.

Surround yourself with supporters

As well as these inner saboteurs, there will be people in your life who will discourage you from making changes. I suggest to clients at this stage of transition to place around them, as much as possible, people who encourage them on their quest to find their vocation. Or

I encourage them to only talk about their dreams to those who support them. In my interviews a couple of men talked about moving from a salaried, well-paid job at midlife to explore different ways of earning a living by setting up their own businesses. They were satisfied with how the change was unfolding but eventually they returned to a salaried job as their wives became anxious about their more precarious work situation. Parents can also discourage a son from making changes. They may express dismay when he gives up his wonderful career of which they are so proud. Clients have also mentioned how, as they plan to leave their work, colleagues will start making comments, even indicating that they must be having a break-down, or are 'gutless', or 'losing the plot'. In fact it is often that their colleagues would love to leave too, and they are projecting onto the person leaving the feelings they have about their own inability to create change in their working life.

BE READY FOR A SURPRISE

Finding a vocation is more about being willing to say yes when one is called. Your Self does the calling and often what you are called to can take you completely by surprise. Often your vocation will be something you never could have imagined as you think back to your attitudes about yourself in the first half of life. For example, Bob, whose midlife story I tell in Chapter 2, told me that he never could have imagined that his vocation at midlife would include working with youth on the street. He never could have envisaged how a path to this vocation could unfold. However, as he remained present to himself, his inner world and to new life experiences, he was guided to it.

TIME OUT IS IMPORTANT

As men begin to realise how dissatisfied they have become with their job, they often feel an urge to take time out. This is understandable and often a message from their psyche for the need to take a rest after so much work pressure. I have observed men take from three months to a couple of years to rebalance and then be ready to find a way to create a different, more personally satisfying contribution through their work. During this time they may still be earning money but their main focus is to create time out for themselves.

YOU HAVE TO BE AN EXPLORER

I have been through three career transitions. Before each change I noticed an increasing dissatisfaction in my present work over a period of at least a couple of years. I have used these couple of years to explore. First I have explored what is going on inside me, and then as ideas come to me about where I might move to next, I go on a quest. As I was becoming less engaged by my organisational consultancy work, and before I started to write, I was considering starting a coaching business. I attended courses, read articles, spoke to others running similar businesses, and even wrote a business plan. At the same time I had an inner voice getting stronger, telling me to write. My inner saboteur kept on saying, 'You can't write'. At the same time as exploring my coaching ideas, I attended a variety of writing workshops, responded to a potential client's request for me to write an article, noticed a significant dream, spoke to a select few about my thoughts and finally started to write. Nobody could have been more surprised than me as my writing career, based on my passion for assisting people at midlife, seemed to then unfold with some ease. I can now see that by continuing to explore my inner world, connecting with my dreams, and taking some personal risks I am now in my vocation. Writing and talking about midlife is not like work. I feel such passion for what I am doing, it resonates so much inside me, I engage with it with ease. I might at times do other work if I feel as though I need to complement my 'vocational income'. I also know that I am at a stage of life where I am willing to simplify so I can put as much of my time as possible into my vocation.

How much do you really need to live on?

As you move towards your vocation you have a decreasing desire for achievements that have little meaning for you. There is also little satisfaction in earning lots of money. As you move into your vocation you know that your satisfaction comes from knowing you are making a difference by contributing to your world from a place deep inside yourself. Certainly you still need to earn a living and fulfil your responsibilities to those around you; however, you also need to balance these responsibilities with your own intrinsic needs. Have you considered how much money you really need to live on? If you found a vocation that deeply fulfilled you, how much would you be willing to forgo financially to pursue it?

Take manageable risks

As you make changes you accommodate yourself if you take manageable risks. If you throw yourself too quickly and at too great a risk into a new situation you may make it too difficult to make adjustments if you realise you have made a wrong turning. In his classic career-change book, *What Color is Your Parachute?*, Nelson Richard Bolles stresses that in the second half of life we need to be aware of how much risk is acceptable for ourselves personally, for what is manageable to one person may be too much for another.

Navigating all the 'tackings and turnings' as you move closer to your vocation is not easy. A willingness to explore, to make time for your inner world and listen to your dreams, and even make wrong turnings is all part of the journey. And once you have found your calling you continue to use these attitudes as your passion for your vocation is renewed and deepened as you live the second half of your life.

CHAPTER 18

childhood abuse, addiction and midlife

I think that people who become slaves to alcohol and other drugs . . .
yearn to go back to Eden. But of course one cannot go back to Eden.
One can only go forward through the painful desert. Addicts are
people who have a more powerful calling than most to the spirit.
They simply have the direction of the journey mixed up.

M. Scott Peck, *Further Along the Road Less Travelled*

FROM MY WORK WITH clients I have come to understand that when people experience serious childhood abuse and neglect it is often much more difficult for them to 'balance their canoe' at midlife. Deep trauma at childhood will mean that much gets repressed into the shadow as one is growing up. When we are young, as socially acceptable parts of the Self remain conscious, the opposite attitudes are pushed back into the unconscious. This weaker side coalesces into the *shadow*. As the contents of the shadow come up from the unconscious at midlife, it can create extreme pain both inwardly and outwardly. Some, especially those who were abused when young, may never be able to meet what is coming up from deep inside them and may remain in the restricted way of being that was developed in the first half of their life. Others, such as Malcolm, turn to substance abuse and other addictions to numb themselves from their extreme inner pain.

Malcolm

I am the eldest of four children. I fought the battles for all of us. Both my parents were alcoholics and they'd scream and yell. We'd hide in the bedroom. Dad was a doctor. He was always moving around with his work. He would beat me up from time to time. Mum would keep us in the bedroom for two to three hours after school until he got home and then he'd beat us. When I was twelve they sat us down and said they were getting divorced. They never did. I wish they had.

When I was young there was lots of inconsistency—sometimes laughter—other times a belt on the back. You never knew whether your behaviour was acceptable or not. It depended on Dad's mood. I learnt to curtail my behaviour and keep my thoughts and feelings to myself. I only shared them with my brother. I learnt to keep the peace. I learnt to try to keep people happy. I learnt to subjugate my own needs. Because there was violence if anything went wrong.

In year 12 I set my goal for my life. I surprised myself and everybody else and got good marks. I decided I wanted to be a successful doctor and parent and to raise my children in a home that knew no arguments. I wanted there to be nothing but consistency and love and to find work and stay there for a long time. This was my idea of a successful life. At twenty, when I was a third-year uni student, and in the middle of exams, my father and I had an argument. He picked up all my notes and threw them down the stairs. After that he tried to hit me. However, he was now smaller than me. I grabbed him by the shirt collar, put him on the floor and said, 'You don't hit me anymore'. Soon afterwards I left home.

I had one girlfriend when young. She lived next door. I didn't really know how to talk to girls. I went to an all-boys' school. In my second year at uni I met my wife. I married her four years later when I finished university. I didn't know what a good lover was. My mum had told me some horror stories about her women friends' sex lives. That was all I had to go on. I had no concept of how male and female relationships should be nor what I should expect because I only had my mum and dad's relationship to go on. I spent my whole married life trying to keep the peace; trying to make everybody happy; not rocking the boat; trying to avoid arguments—just as I'd done when I was a kid.

When I married, my parents were very critical of my wife and when my son was born there was no recognition from them of his birth. After that I made the decision to have nothing to do with my father and mother because otherwise I couldn't achieve the goal with my family of having no conflict. So I didn't see my family, including my siblings, as I couldn't lock out one without the other.

When I got to my mid-thirties my wife's parents died and that was a huge change in the dynamics of the family. My parents-in-law had treated me as one of their own and gave me the love I had never had from my own parents. For me it was like the death of the father and mother I had always wanted. It was at this time I became conscious that I was 'working my arse off'. I had no life of my own. I'd achieved the nice house, the nice car, a wife who appeared to be everything a man could want. However, I wasn't happy. It was costing me so much working 55 hours a week. I wondered, 'Where is the joy in life?' My wife threw herself into the family and things weren't good between us. When I got home at night after work she and the kids would have eaten. So all I was doing was going to work and coming home, eating by myself in the kitchen. I didn't feel part of it. They were happy because of what I was doing but there wasn't any joy in it for me. It especially grated for me not sharing the family meal together. I felt I was living somebody else's life, somebody else's dream. I started to drink. I felt alienated and lonely. Then communication was so bad between my wife and I that I'd stay up late playing computer games. My wife would ask me when I was coming to bed. The saddest thing is that I'd hug my wife while she was asleep because I couldn't do it while she was awake.

Then I started smoking dope, something I hadn't done since my early twenties. I was 41. At weekends I'd say I was going swimming and go to a park and have a few joints and feel how trapped I was in my life and then swim a few laps and when I had red eyes from the dope they thought it was from the swimming. I would be away from home for three to four hours and the family would wonder why. Then during the week I'd say I was going to medical meetings. I'd check that there was one on so I had an alibi. Then I'd smoke a few joints and go to a movie. Towards the end of the marriage I'd get up early in the morning, go to the park, walk in the frost and fog, and have a joint before work. I felt that if I'd died under a tree nobody would know or care. This was a really low point. It was six months after this that my marriage ended. I went to a conference and met a woman. Nothing physical happened between us, but we kept in touch by email. We would sometimes meet and go to the movies. I had a sense that somebody cared about me as a person. Also the clandestine aspect of it brought some excitement into my otherwise depressing life. I thought it was justifiable to myself because we didn't have intercourse and so it wasn't an affair because I still had strong morals re cheating and going behind my wife's back. At this time I was totally locked into a ten-hour working day.

And then one Sunday I said I was going swimming but I visited her and we became closer. Just as I was walking out my wife rang on the mobile asking where I was. Driving home I thought, 'This can't go on. My life is in tatters. I'm working my arse off, swallowing whatever pills are there.' I got home and walked in the front door and said, 'I'm leaving', as I knew sooner or later I'd get caught in a compromising position. I packed my bag and stayed with my brother-in-law for a week while I searched for a flat to live in. I saw this week as a window of opportunity when she could have said, 'Let's talk'. I was waiting for her to show some expression of care. She didn't. It made me feel very unimportant in her and the family's life.

Since I left my marriage, life has been an absolute roller-coaster. Initially I was exhilarated with the newfound freedom. In the seven months before the marriage ended we hadn't made love once. A month after I moved into a flat I started a sexual relationship with my friend and we made love every day for six months. After eighteen months she started talking about wanting children. I said no. I'd had a vasectomy. She was persistent and problems started arising between us as I could see she wanted the nice family and house which I had already done. At the same time I had a lot of pressure on me through the Family Court and I was still working a 55-hour week. My weight dropped significantly. On legal advice I eventually had to sell out of my medical practice, although it had been my life, so as to separate my life from my wife's.

The court cases were massive. They went on for two and a half years and just about caused me a nervous breakdown. I ended up manic, excitable, agitated, restless, garrulous. It looked to me that the way the Family Court was handling things I was going to lose everything that I had built up over twenty years. I didn't see my children for twelve months after seeing them daily. I'd lost my wife. I thought I'd also lost my kids. And the Family Court was making sure I lost most of my assets. It was as though the last twenty years were completely nullified. Everything I'd brought into my life was going.

At 44 years I started seeing a psychologist and a psychiatrist as well. I realised I was suffering from depression and probably had been for a long time. And I started trying to do something to deal with the depression. I saw the psychologist weekly for counselling and I saw the psychiatrist monthly. He put me on antidepressants. For me to admit I had an emotional health problem was a pretty big step.

Since the separation I now have no goals, hopes, dreams or ambitions. Everything I wanted to achieve in life I've already achieved. I've done it. I had the wife, family and house and I still wasn't happy. I don't want those things anymore but that leaves a big hole. And at this point in life I don't know what I want. Three months ago I was very low again because I realised I had no purpose in life. I felt my life was over. Lately I've just been realising I need to find a new reason for living and I haven't yet found it. Yet the one thing I have found is that I'm not as worried about not having a reason for living. So for the last couple of months I've been a little more content because I've just changed my attitude. That the day-to-day things that happen in life might be the reason for living. I don't necessarily have to have a long-term goal, sometimes you just have to live.

In the last six months I've started to address my alcohol and drug dependency problem. Two consecutive days a week are drug- and alcohol-free. For now a minimum goal for me is to take better care of myself. I also play squash once a week. I still have my down times and have a long way to go on my journey but I think I've been through the 'eye of the storm' and through the clouds I can see a glimmer of sunshine. And maybe the sun will come out again and maybe it won't, but for the moment I'll just hold onto that little bit of sunshine that's in my life from day to day and not worry too much about what the future holds.

Another midlife experience for me has been dealing with arthritis in my hands. I've had to learn to adjust to bodily deterioration. At midlife I've faced my own mortality and morbidity. At 47 I look and feel like a 34-year-old. I have to realise I'm getting older and I don't want to—a bit of a Peter Pan really. But the arthritis in my hands reminds me of my age. I have seen some friends and acquaintances die over the years and I wonder about my own death. It's not dying that scares me. It's how I get there.

When my marriage ended I lost all my friends and family, which really showed me the depths of those friendships. It was so easy for my wife to say that I ran away with another woman. But the upside of that is that I have made new friends. We've shared our ups and downs and they know me as I truly am. Without the support of these friendships in the last few years I wouldn't have made it. That includes most of all my brother who I hadn't seen for twenty years. I'm also lucky that some of the women I've had relationships with have become friends. It's the first time I've had women who are just friends. After I left my marriage I fell into relationships without thinking about them. Anybody who made me feel valuable I'd readily accept into my life. But I still had this in-built thing of not rocking the boat no matter what the cost. I also very strongly believe that every woman who has come into my life has given me a gift. I have had several relationships since separating—it's the learning I didn't get to do in adolescence. I didn't have a clue as to what sort of woman would suit me. I didn't have good role models. I have now got to know women as people. I now know that any relationship I have in the future will have to serve my needs. And if my needs aren't fulfilled in a relationship I'm better off without them. Therefore, while I'm the sort of guy who loves to be in a relationship I've learnt I'm better without one unless it is right for me.

I ended a relationship totally upset. I'd invested a lot in it. It was a difficult one to end. At the end of it, when I arrived back at my home there was an outpouring of, 'I'm no good at relationships. What do I have to do to find somebody who will love me?' I got three large pieces of paper and wrote down:

- Some benefits of choosing to be single.
- If you need a woman you don't really need a woman.
- The words from a song by Alanis Morissette, 'That I would be good'.

It helped me release my emotions. I knew the relationship was damaging both of us. I wasn't in a good head space during it.

I was emotionally unwell. So I was examining the possibility of remaining single, realising that a relationship wasn't the answer to my difficulties. I needed to do work on myself. But it still took two years from then to really be able to spend time by myself out of a relationship. I now know that happiness won't come from a woman making me happy. Happiness has to come from my internal understanding of myself. I'm still not through my midlife upheaval.

ACKNOWLEDGING INNER PAIN AT MIDLIFE

As you read Malcolm's story were there any aspects of his childhood and midlife journey that resonated with your own? All children experience some 'wounding' when young. In its extreme it becomes abuse. At midlife Malcolm's psyche encouraged him to connect with inner pain that was there as a result of childhood abuse. He numbed himself from this inner pain by smoking marijuana, drinking alcohol and taking medication he had easy access to as a doctor. He is now taking steps to reduce these addictions. Have you any addictions? They need not be as severe as Malcolm's. Anything we do often to avoid our inner pain can become an addiction. Workaholism, pornography, gambling and drinking alcohol are four of the most prevalent addictions among men in our society. Our society even reinforces workaholism as it applauds men who work long hours.

Before Malcolm's 'midlife crisis' he was working 55 hours a week. Unfortunately this is all too common in our society and in fact overwork is a man's acceptable addiction. Whether it is an addiction depends on the motive of and the effect of a man spending all this time at work. A man may use the busyness of work as a way of avoiding the pain inside himself. Any addiction also impacts on one's ability to maintain close relationships and so another way of telling whether a working life contains elements of workaholism is to ask oneself: 'Is my work impacting on my ability to maintain close relationships with those I love?'

At times, as men are providing an affluent lifestyle for their families, they feel locked in by all the financial expectations on them. Do you feel locked in financially by your family's financial expectations on you? Would you consider changing your and your family's lifestyle to take some of the financial pressure off you and give you some time for yourself? Perhaps to give yourself time to deal with some of your inner pain.

When wanting to deal with an addiction, we need to look at our self-limiting thoughts. These messages keep us safe when young; however, as adults they are no longer necessary, nor do they serve us. Malcolm learnt as a child to keep the peace; to try to keep people happy; and to subjugate his own needs. These were still guiding principles for him as he entered midlife. When young he had learnt that if anything went wrong either he or one of his siblings was abused by his parents. Until he finds a way to work through this fear he will find it difficult not to be controlled by these inner, now self-limiting messages.

In many ways these guiding principles served Malcolm well in the first half of his life. They helped him to create a family life where he could feel secure. But in the long run they were also part of his undoing. He is now gradually learning to not live by these messages; however, this will take much work, for these messages or rules for survival are deeply entrenched in a person who has experienced childhood abuse.

Malcolm is also grappling with his dependency on a relationship with a woman. This is a challenge for men at midlife. Until a man has developed his inner feminine, learnt to take care of himself physically, learnt how to have nurturing, intimate relationships, he will remain very dependent on having a female partner to provide this for him.

Below you will find 'Malcolm's list of some benefits of choosing to be single'. As Malcolm says, he is pleased to have had the relationships he has had since separation and divorce as he is now acquiring the relationship skills others learn much earlier. Luckily it is never too late to do the developmental work we might have missed out on earlier. That is what Malcolm is doing now.

Malcolm's list of some benefits of choosing to be single

- *You can please yourself.*
- *You don't have to please another unless you want to.*
- *You can go out with lots of girls.*
- *You can go out with lots of guys.*
- *You can go out with whoever you like.*
- *You can stay home and be quiet and peaceful.*
- *You don't upset anyone you have to live with.*
- *You don't say rotten things to someone you love.*
- *You never need to be jealous or angry.*
- *You don't rely on any one person to give you love or make you feel worthwhile.*
- *You can truly learn to be yourself.*
- *You can't blame anyone else for your problems.*
- *You can experiment and have to prove nothing.*
- *You can live up to your own expectations.*
- *You don't add anyone's traumas and life's difficulties to your own.*
- *There can be no misunderstanding.*
- *Your partner doesn't have sudden unexpected mood swings.*
- *No-one else but you is responsible for your happiness.*

PART 5

Your inner compass helps you navigate

In the second half of life, our old compasses no longer work.
The new compass that we need cannot be held in our hand, only in our heart.
We read it not with our mind alone, but with our soul.

Mark Gerzon, *Listening to Midlife*

CHAPTER 19

spiritual awakening
at midlife

The Self archetype can be described in psychological terms as an
inner guiding factor and one can experience the expression of this Self
in quiet, meditative moments: for example, as an inner voice.

Dr Peter O'Connor, *Understanding Jung*

ON A COLD WINTER'S day in my mid-thirties I decided to light
a fire and just sit. I had taken long service leave from my part-time
job as an educational psychologist and my three young children were
at school and family day care. It was a very unusual thing for me
to do; first of all to light a fire, and secondly to just sit. My days and
evenings were usually spent on myriad activities. My life was full
of busyness.

As I sat it felt very uncomfortable and unfamiliar. I felt heavy and
sad. I sat and the more I sat, the heavier I felt. My body was aching.
I kept on sitting and the more I noticed 'me' the more I realised that
all these sensations were constantly there. For the rest of the morning
I vacillated between sitting still and noticing my inner state, and
reading rather distractedly. And since then a string of events has
followed that makes me believe that from that moment on I was

consciously in contact with something new and important—my inner voice, my inner guide, my spiritual Self.

My understanding of spirituality

Spirituality is an often-used, if not overused word. Before I continue I will explain what spirituality means to me. Spirituality is when I turn my attention to my inner life and become aware of my inner world. Turning my attention to my inner world is an expression of the feminine side of my nature. My inner feminine allows me to wait patiently, listening for my inner voice and to the wisdom that comes from my inner feminine feeling and intuition. As I connect with this I connect with my spiritual Self. This in turn connects me to an inner knowing; a sense of purpose and meaning to my life that increasingly involves an aspect of service to the greater whole and a feeling of greater connection to all around me—to people, animals, nature, the earth, the universe.

Connecting with inner feelings and intuition

Sitting with myself on that cold winter's day started me on an inner journey. Soon afterwards my inner voice led me to learn meditation, a practice which reinforced my inner focus. There are many different forms of meditation and the one I learnt in my mid-thirties at this time of spiritual awakening was one where I used a mantra to still my mind. As I started to meditate twice a day—once in the early morning and then in the late afternoon—I discovered a place of deep relaxation and tranquillity. Sometimes I connected with unsettling feelings and even started crying, and that was fine too. Over the next six months meditation became an important part of my life and although I didn't realise why at the time, I felt I was being guided in my life as I awoke to my spiritual Self.

Inner feelings guide us to our spiritual Self

It wasn't until I started writing my first book that I realised that the turbulent feelings I had experienced at midlife were vital for my own psychological and spiritual development, as once processed they lead me to all the wisdom of my spiritual Self. For example, in my mid to late thirties I experienced lethargy as my psyche encouraged me to slow down, spend time with myself and go within to find out more about my own true nature. As I honoured my feelings I connected with my intuition which I experienced as an inner voice or as an inner knowing about what I needed to do. As I learnt to trust my feelings and intuition, I learnt to trust my most important guide, my spiritual Self. My inner voice eventually led me to other practices that have been used throughout the centuries for spiritual awakening. Practices such as writing, drawing, dancing, singing and all forms of creative pursuits—all of these can lead to an experience of Self, of spirit. As I connected to my inner feelings and intuition I also became aware of another guide in my life—synchronicity.

Synchronicity is a guide at midlife

Have you ever had the experience of thinking of a business acquaintance you haven't thought of, seen or spoken to in a long time, when the phone rings and there he is? Or you have been wondering how you might come by some important information, when you walk into a friend's office, and there it is on his desk. Or perhaps at a time when you needed guidance you had an astrological or tarot reading, or dabbled in numerology. If so, you have been tapping into what Jung coined 'synchronicity'.

As I connected with my inner world in my mid-thirties I noticed a strange happening in my life. It was as though once I started to ask myself soul-searching questions, answers presented themselves to me in my outer world, as long as I remained vigilant to it. I experienced moments of truth and intuitive knowing. Looking back I can now see that as a result of this first awareness of synchronistic events with the ensuing feelings, I was led to an energy and passion for activities and to a potential I had never previously suspected. I felt as though I was being led down a path to a new purpose and meaning to my life. Since then I have often experienced what I now understand to be synchronicity and I have found that at midlife it has been an invaluable guide. I will give an example from my own life to explain what I mean.

One day while meditating in those first few months I suddenly came to the understanding I should go on a holiday without my family while on long service leave from my current job as an educational psychologist. It was a very unusual thing for me to do as I left three young children at home.

On the holiday, the events that happened were:

1   I went scuba diving for the first time. At the practice session in the hotel pool I had nearly fainted while underwater. I fainted often as a child, especially when fearful, and so I had to overcome significant fear and anxiety to take the first dive into the ocean. After that first day of diving I stood on the prow of the boat and leant into the wind thinking to myself, 'I can do anything if I just put my mind to it'.

2   At the holiday resort there were several businessmen who, I gradually realised, appreciated being able to talk over with me their work problems. Towards the end of the holiday while talking with one of them I had this fleeting thought, 'I would be as bright if not brighter than these men. I am just as articulate, if not more so. I also probably have more formal qualifications. Why is it that they are doing more interesting, challenging, well-paid work with much greater recognition?'

3   On the following morning while having breakfast, my friend Tess turned to me and said, 'I think you will do something

special with your work one day'. I was nonplussed. Her comment came out of the blue. I had not mentioned any of my inner thoughts to her. I was barely aware of them myself.

4   I had a prophetic daydream while flying back home. I put headphones on, lay back, closed my eyes and relaxed into the music. Suddenly I had a vision of myself speaking in front of a large group of people. I was dressed in a black dress and a bright jacket. It was 'corporate' dress. I hadn't ever dressed that way. As soon as I came out of this daydream I started planning a new professional life.

5   As soon as I got home from holiday I started being proactive in creating this professional life. However, one day I started to question inwardly whether it was possible to make the transition from the education sector to setting up my own business in the corporate sector. As I was walking down the street wondering about this, I bumped into a woman I had met several years beforehand at a course. I asked about her life and she told me that six months beforehand she had left her job as a psychologist in the education sector, had spent six months working in a local consultancy firm, and was now working with one of the country's top consultancies. I had the answer. It was possible.

As you read the above account you might have been saying to yourself, 'So what!' However, I was very aware there was something new happening in my life. It felt as if I was being led down a path. All I had to do was ask a question, then look for the signposts to check I had read the signs properly.

Jung was the first person to give synchronicity psychological meaning. The simplest definition that Jung gave synchronicity was 'a meaningful coincidence'. When we say something is 'meaningful' we usually mean it has touched one of our core values or it has had a big impact on our lives. A meaningful event might have one or both of these attributes. Synchronistic events move us deeply because there is a simultaneous occurrence of a certain psychological state within us with one or more external events that are meaningfully connected to our inner state.

In the above example, my internal, emotional state and inner questioning about my work was reflected in the chance occurrence in the outer world when Tess said out of the blue that she thought I would do something special in my work one day. Similarly, when I was walking along the street wondering whether it was possible to make my planned work transition, my emotional, questioning state was reflected in the external event of the chance meeting with an old acquaintance showing me it was possible. In both these cases my inner thoughts were meaningfully connected with outer events in my world.

CHARACTERISTICS OF SYNCHRONICITY

In both of the above examples it was a chance occurrence that these people said what they did at the time. If they had known previously about my inner questioning, it would not be a coincidence. And this coincidental nature along with its meaningfulness for us is what makes something synchronistic. When I experience synchronicity I have found certain characteristics present.

First, a new understanding becomes conscious to me. For instance, in relation to the previous example, I had only ever thought of working for another employer or working as a counsellor in private practice. Second, I am stretched to perceive myself in a different way. After my experiences of scuba diving, talking to businessmen and having my prophetic daydream I started to assess myself as capable of more than I had previously imagined. My mind started opening up to possibilities I had never thought possible. Third, I notice further events that help reinforce I am on the right track. Just as I was questioning if it was possible to make the transition, an acquaintance appeared to demonstrate to me it was possible. Fourth, synchronicity has occurred at points of important transition or a turning point in my life. Fifth, as I become more aware of my own core values I am more likely to notice synchronicity in my life. And finally, synchronicity is a valuable guide for me as I navigate midlife transition. My teachers are all around me.

SPIRITUAL TEACHERS ARE ALL AROUND US

In my quest to understand my own spiritual awakening at midlife, Carl Jung's teachings helped me enormously. However, these days I accept my spiritual teachers are all around me. If I keep open-minded as I go about my life, I develop my spiritual understandings as I ask myself questions about all I experience. The questing, the quest, the search is my spiritual teacher. As long as I continue to connect to my inner world I will be led to what I need for my own spiritual development.

As I notice my own thoughts, read books, listen to the radio, go to public talks, talk with friends and attend courses I notice that certain ideas have energy for me. As I grapple with all the ups and downs of my life I keep in mind others' understandings and discern which ones help me. Whenever I tap into another's understandings, whether they be a recognised spiritual teacher, another writer, a speaker or a friend, I actively think about what they are saying, turn it over, and see if it fits for me. Some understandings I reject as not useful for me, perhaps to return to later. Or perhaps I believe a certain understanding or practice will never be a useful guidepost to help me along my spiritual path. So I find it is the befriending of myself as I move through my day that offers me the best teacher and guide to my spiritual life. As I have insights about myself and my life I 'learn on the job'. Certain understandings become mine as I learn through trial and error. As I take in new information I reflect on what is being said, actively question, and then notice if it helps me on my spiritual path. I am only willing to adopt truths I have person-ally experienced. If I am to do this my greatest challenge is be truly present to myself and my everyday experiences.

For example, when reading Robert Sardello's book, *Freeing the Soul from Fear*, I was very drawn to his concept of creative love. He describes creative love as the mode of love that has the power to transform human beings as spirit is recognised in a brief encounter. Sardello says that, 'In creative love, the smallest act of love released into the world produces the same result as the largest act of love released into the world'. A couple of days after reading about creative love I was a member of an a cappella group that sang and danced down a people-lined street for over a couple of hours as part of a festival. It was at a time of serious unrest in the Middle East and I was aware that there were many people in the crowd from this region and I felt compassion for them. As I sang and danced I felt fully alive and open and I enjoyed making eye contact with others as we moved down the street. After a while I made eye contact with a young Middle Eastern woman and I felt an expression of love pass between us. It is a moment I will never forget. For me, this was an experience of Sardello's creative love. I could now move beyond an intellectual understanding of creative love to the conscious experience of it.

OUR OWN SPIRITUAL TRUTHS

All teachings, although taking different roads, lead us to some universal truths that are signposts on our own spiritual journey. As long as we continue to understand ourselves, our true nature, we are led to these truths. In the past fifteen years as I have befriended my spiritual Self I have come to accept certain spiritual truths about my life. Others before may have expressed them; however, I know them to be true for me through my own experience. Before you read some of my personal spiritual truths you might like to grab a pen and paper and write some of your own. Like mine, your list will not be definitive but just by doing the exercise you can increase your awareness of some of the spiritual truths you are living your life by. I suggest you find somewhere relaxing, give yourself at least half an hour, and see what you come up with. I have found it an interesting exercise to share with friends and family.

My personal spiritual truths

- My daily life presents me with all the lessons I need for my own spiritual development.
- Life wasn't meant to be easy.
- If I communicate openly, honestly and respectfully with all those around me I will be rewarded with a deepening understanding of myself and what is right for me in my life.
- You get back what you put in. Not necessarily immediately, but at some stage.
- I need to learn the same lessons time and time again.
- Love conquers all.
- As I spiritually grow, my life gets better and better.
- My most important spiritual guide is within me.

We all face the challenge of how to bring spirituality into our everyday life and we will all find our own unique way to do this at midlife. We search for guidance. But which path do we take? One of my friends feels supported on her spiritual path as she regularly visits India to be in the presence of Sai Baba; others are Buddhists; some are part of a church congregation; others are part of various societies that follow certain spiritual teachings and practices. Whatever our practices, our challenge is to live a life that mirrors the spiritual understandings that support us to reflect our own inner spirit. To meet this challenge we must deal with the struggles life presents us with and then do the personal work to transform and break down the barriers we built within ourselves during the first half of life. We develop the skills to communicate openly with all those around us— our children, our partners, our colleagues, our friends; we discover how to contribute to society in a meaningful way; we strive to make every aspect of our life a reflection of our spiritual Self; we move towards wholeness.

As I move into the second half of my life I believe that as long as I continue the practices that befriend my Self, I will be led to what I need for my ongoing spiritual journey. I read and listen to others' understandings and teachings; however, I choose what feels right for me at this time of my life as I paddle my canoe. My spiritual teachers are all around me, but most importantly my best spiritual teacher and guide is within me.

CHAPTER 20

clarifying your values

It is the spirit within us, found in the core of our own
Selves, that slowly and painfully weaves its way
through anxiety, confusion, tension, and conflict
to hear the rhythm of our own personal tune made
up of choices and values that are truly our own.

A. Brennan & J. Brewi, *Mid-Life: Psychological and Spiritual Perspectives*

AT MIDLIFE IT IS important to find ways to gain clarity about our core values. As we enter midlife transition we connect with our 'selves' from both stages—the previous conditioned self and the evolving authentic Self. We also connect with the values from both stages. It can be a very bewildering and challenging time for us and those around us as we move from a life based on values that are more outwardly focused, family and work oriented, to inner, more personally centred values.

This chapter contains the final part of my initial interview with Michael. One of the things he talks about is the importance, for him, of clarifying his values as he made his difficult and important midlife decisions. As you read you might like to consider how clear you are about your own core values, and what regular practices you might be willing to put in place to ensure you are making changes that reflect those core values as you navigate midlife.

Michael: I notice there are situations when I am closed. Over the years I have developed a lot of sensitivity and indicators to show me very quickly that I am closed. Then I can do something about it. There are areas in normal life where people can stay closed for weeks or months. Some people stay closed for years. And the more we are closed down the less we are available to our life, so I don't want to be closed down.

Robyn: So what sort of things would you now notice that show you are closing down?

Michael: If I notice myself pulling back from engaging with others or becoming defensive during the day I do something about it. I may not be able to do anything with it straight away. I may be in a meeting or something but I make a mental note and I do come back to it.

Robyn: How long have you done that for? Do you remember when you first started doing it?

Michael: It was in my mid-thirties. It was an important step for me. As you know from your own experience, sometimes your life presents you with situations or feelings where it feels like absolute death. It feels shocking. Out of so many experiences I now know it's never as horrible as the fear tells me it will be.

Robyn: What are some of the things you do to work out what the fear is about?

Michael: I use a variety of artistic means—sometimes I draw or do clay modelling. I also write a lot. I have always kept a journal. I write a lot of my thoughts and feelings down and by doing so a lot of things become clear. It is a process that will never be finished. But I feel I am so much more in touch with myself, more connected to myself than I have ever been. And there is a long way to go and that's okay. I have a few incarnations to go so I don't have to achieve everything this time around.

From my early thirties I was involved in a lot of men's groups for a period of ten years. There was a lot of discussion around things that particularly pertain to men. For example, the men there would talk about wanting to break out of the restrictions of having a mortgage but nobody actually did anything about it. It was seen as an absolute burden. When I left the business world I made it publicly known why I was leaving and in my farewell speeches I stated very clearly what was going on for me and a lot of people in quite senior positions came and said, 'I wish I could do that too. I hate the bloody mortgage.' And I said, 'Look, you may forget about me but before you sign on the dotted line for your next mortgage just think about me and think, "Is that really what I want to do?" ' That's the name of the game. The mortgage locks you in.

Now I have changed career again. I have left management completely and made a shift towards therapeutic work. This is an even bigger shift because I am moving into an area that is fairly unfamiliar to me and in many ways I am as yet unskilled. So in my early fifties I am stepping into a totally new space. I am wanting to give back to the world, to be of service.

Robyn: So that would be a fairly strong value, a strong priority—to be able to work in a way that you are giving back.

Michael: Absolutely. And in many ways the career shift I started eight years ago when I left the business sector was completed last year when I finally left my management role at my present workplace.

Robyn: So that was like an in-between transition time.

Michael: Yes. I now have no interest in being involved in management. It's gone.

Robyn: The literature would suggest that during midlife transition it is vital we clarify our core values and use these to shape the second half of our life. Are you aware of other values besides wanting to be of service?

Michael: Yes, I have a refined system of values which I review very regularly. For me to joyfully be of service is a key value. Another value is that whatever I do I want to leave other people free. This doesn't mean I don't sometimes hurt other people. Sometimes by being truthful it is hurtful but it depends on the motive.

Robyn: So is this around the area of control, when you talk about leaving people free?

Michael: Yes, I want to respect people's own journey. I don't want to control people.

Robyn: That is very different from how you described yourself as being twenty years ago when you were controlling and not even aware of it. So now consciously you want to make sure you are not.

Michael: Yes. I am not controlling and I am not controlled. I want to be free and I don't want to impinge on the freedom of others. I have to be like this, especially in my therapeutic work. The other value is to operate out of trust. And the other value high on my list is to be truthful. This does not only mean to not tell lies but also to speak things that may be difficult to speak. If to be true to my values something needs to be spoken, I need to speak it. Hopefully I do this in a way that leaves other people to do the same.

I do a lot of work around values. These are general statements but for me behind each one there are chapters around which I regularly question myself. In the last ten years I have taken five days at the beginning of each year to go camping. I don't see anybody and I spend the time reviewing the year. So at the beginning of each year I write down my aims and goals and values and at the end of the year I see how I have scored against that. I then decide what I want to carry on with and what I want to let go of. For me that regular review process at least once a year is very important.

Robyn: It's valuable isn't it. It's not just a focusing thing. It is also an acknowledgment of the changes you have made. Because it is very easy to make changes and not notice and to just move on to the next thing.

Michael: Yes. And what I want to guard against is just drifting through the years. Life can be so hectic. I don't want to just drift through my life and then realise a few years down the track, 'Shit, this isn't where I want to be'.

Robyn: You want to make sure you are steering your own canoe?

Michael: Yes.

Robyn: And it's your values that guide you, if you are aware of them and keep them conscious.

Michael: Yes. So for me I review every day to see how much I have been able to live life in a way to be true to my values. For me my highest goal, my highest value is my personal integrity and that is dependent on how much I am able to live my daily life in accordance with my values. And there are some days when I do better than other days. I feel I am now at a fascinating time, having let go of my long-term relationship and my main career—my new work position will probably disappear at the end of the year but it doesn't worry me. I don't want to lock myself in—and I want to trust— and I am in no hurry to close down the uncertainty. I am very happy to live with that. It's fascinating to be open, like a totally new chapter starting up.

Robyn: It's a bit like starting a totally new life isn't it? Although you made a big transition eight years ago it is another one now.

Michael: Yes. And now I earn a fraction of what I earned, but it doesn't matter. I now don't have anybody to support as my children are now independent financially. It is up to me to decide how much I need to live. I can live on very little. And I trust enough will be there. It feels exciting. A big difference for me now from when I left the business sector is that now I know exactly what I want to do. I know where my passion is, where my heart is, whereas back then I didn't have a clue.

Robyn: So this is your passion now?

Michael: Yes. My passion is to work with people in a therapeutic way. I have a lot to learn. This year I am learning heaps and that is fantastic. The feedback I am getting is quite good. I am getting involved in a variety of work, it's all learning, it's all great. So that is where my passion is. And there are a few other aspects I have to think through in the next six months. I am involved in quite a few boards using my old skills in strategic thinking and strategic planning and I have to think about whether I want to keep on doing them.

Robyn: From the look on your face it's as though you are feeling, 'This isn't me anymore'. But it takes a while to let go of all those things, doesn't it.

Michael: Yes.

Robyn: It's interesting, isn't it, that the things we could do years ago with a lot of energy now don't have the same appeal. It's not that you can't do it. It's just that you don't have the same will. Your energy wants to go elsewhere.

Michael: Yes, like when I left the business world. However, it can be very difficult for others, especially those close to you. I was quite contented but one of my sons who was sixteen at the time was very angry with me for a long time. Years later he told me the biggest problem was when his friends asked, 'What is your dad doing?' I'd been in a senior position in a prestigious company, now I was living in a commune and doing volunteer work. He was utterly embarrassed because it was at a time when he was trying to find his own identity and he had looked at me as the role model. I had pulled the rug out from underneath him.

Robyn: While he's going through his identity crisis at adolescence you are going through yours. Which is often the case. There can be a lot of difficulties between parents and children because they are both going through turbulent times.

Michael: It was difficult to be confronted with the very clear needs and demands made of me by the family. No doubt a normal family man would behave in a way to look after the family's needs first and there I was very clearly putting my own needs and values first. I was putting my needs higher than the family's needs and that was a difficult phase and the family members could not understand.

Robyn: You haven't got any parents here in Australia have you? Do you think it would have made any difference if you'd had your parents living around the corner?

Michael: No.

Robyn: So there was nobody who could make you feel guilty enough
to make you stay where you were?

Michael: No. My immediate family tried and I took that very seriously.
I had to question myself very hard: 'Why am I doing this?' because
you don't risk giving pain to them for something not well thought
through.

Robyn: You wanted to make sure you were on the right track.

Michael: I felt it was something essential for me. I could make compromises right, left and centre which didn't bother me but I had to be
true to myself. And that's what the family couldn't understand.
The family's needs always had to come first. A good father would
never jeopardise the combined goodwill of the family, just for
himself. And that was a value difference. And I do need to say
I take my family responsibilities very seriously but there is something higher for me than the needs of the family.

Robyn: But you are also talking about needs of the family that you
might also say aren't so important. Like their discomfort about the
type of job you do. Because you would still consider the family's
needs, wouldn't you.

Michael: Yes. Absolutely. They are very difficult decisions when you
put your values higher than those people you love very much.

VALUES CLARIFICATION AT MIDLIFE

If we are constantly in busyness mode, we do not have time to reflect
on whether we are spending our time on the things that most matter
to us. Life is giving us choices all the time and they are not easy to
make, especially if we are not conscious of our core values, and
the priority in which we place them. What are your values? The
first step in discovering our core values is to go within. In our quieter,
more reflective moments, answers will come to us about what we
most value. These answers might come symbolically through dreams,
daydreams or writing. The second step is to observe ourselves,
how we feel physically, emotionally, intellectually and spiritually as

we move through our day. What engages us? What energises us? What do we find most fulfilling? As we develop the practices to connect with our Self we gradually get a sense of what feels right deep inside us.

Values clarification exercise

To help you get in contact with your core values I would like you to imagine a hypothetical situation. Your doctor has just told you that you have a life-threatening illness. Physically you will remain quite able; however, there is nothing medically that can be done, and within a year you could be dead. Find a comfortable, distraction-free place to sit and close your eyes. Spend some time imaging yourself in this situation. When you open your eyes, list on a piece of paper up to ten of the most important things that come to mind that you would want to have in your life in that twelve months. If you have done this exercise with an open mind you have touched values that are truly important to you. And it is these values that can light your way on your midlife journey.

CHAPTER 21

relish every moment

*Awareness is found in our pleasure and our
pain, our confusion and our wisdom, available in
each moment of our weird, unfathomable,
ordinary everyday lives.*

Pema Chodron, *When Things Fall Apart*

EACH DAY WE ARE given opportunities to learn more about our own true nature, yet much of the time we do not take advantage of them. When finding ourselves in an uncomfortable situation, we unconsciously switch off from it by distracting ourselves with busyness, with addictions, with anything that will stop us from being present to our inner discomfort. Through meditation we develop a gentle kindness towards all our own feelings and thoughts. We learn to notice them, to acknowledge them, and then to let them go. We learn to notice when we shut down and so no longer do we shut down in ignorance. We see very clearly when we are closing off, and through this noticing we learn more about our fears, our hopes, our own true nature. As we develop the practice of meditating daily this supports us to be more awake to ourselves in the midst of our everyday life. We start to relax within the presence of all our feelings and thoughts, no longer do we struggle with ourselves, we are increasingly able to stay present to the moment.

Manny

I was born a severe haemophiliac. I am 51 now so there wasn't any treatment for it when I was young. I'd have bleeding episodes I couldn't control and there was severe pain; however, from a very early age I was aware that there was something I could do to take the pain away.

Eight years ago, when the kids were eight, ten and twelve, my wife, Jenny, got a melanoma. We were told that if it didn't come back for five years she would probably be okay. After four years it did. We went to a ten-day residential program at the Gawler Foundation where I realised that what I had been doing all my life to manage my pain was a form of meditation.

When Jenny was dying I had to look for some meaning in the whole thing. I was thinking there must be something greater to come out of it than all this shit. There was a major shift in me one morning while meditating. I just came to terms with it all. I was able to take the positives out of the process my wife was going through. She was ready to die. I was sort of uplifted by the process she went through. All that I went through around Jenny's dying and my time at the Gawler Foundation showed me that it's the state of your mind when you die that is important, not when you die. I'm sure Buddhists and Jews and other religions feel the same way. It's not living a long life that is important, it's being happy with my life at any one moment.

Four months after Jenny died I had a hip replacement operation. I then got an infection and had to be in hospital for four months. I had ten operations in three months. I was out of hospital for six months before getting another infection and going back in for another four months. I nearly died a couple of times during all of this, yet I felt in the back of my mind it was all going to be okay.

So in the middle of my forties I had two years that were really shit: my wife dying and then me being in hospital much of the time. While all of this was going on meditation helped me put all my emotions together and keep all the pieces of my life together. I look at meditation similar to how some people view praying. It's just like contemplating. I find that if I regularly spend time just being with myself it helps me know exactly where I am at any moment of the day—my feelings and where I am in the whole picture of all the people who are important to me—my kids, my partner, my friends. There is a purpose for every meeting in my day and I relish every moment. I don't treat any other moment as more important than the other—they're all important. However, it is not just meditation that has helped me with this. Living alongside my wife as she was dying made me see a bit more of the big picture and then meditation reinforced it all.

I don't have a regular practice of meditation. I don't get up at six and do it every morning, although I will often take fifteen minutes during the day to just sit. I also give myself pauses during the day, say a minute or two, to assess how I'm feeling in a situation. I'll stop and focus and this helps me to sense what is happening inside me. I find it helps me deal with everything much better, especially those situations that are upsetting me. Since starting these practices six years ago I don't have the anxiety I used to have.

I now go to a group meditation one night a week. It's the same group I went to with Jenny. All the other participants have or have had cancer. Most are in their thirties and forties. It's amazing to share the experiences people have when they are looking death in the face. They have thought themselves well, then they find out they have cancer. For some they find they are to die soon. Then they go to a place where they are not worrying anymore about finding a cure, they are just looking within for the answers— it is wonderful to be able to observe this. They start enjoying a rose, or a cloud or a greeting—all those things they'd ignored because they'd been so caught up with all the other stuff. They realise they've been busy seeking this stuff that doesn't really bring them any joy.

In my mid-forties I started a support group for severe haemophiliacs. They are all about my age. They've all had bad legs like me and half of them have HIV because of all the blood trans-fusions. Because we are older there really isn't much support outside in the health system anymore. So we have created our own support. We get together once every six weeks to talk about what is happening in our lives.

I'm different from lots of other guys my age. I tend to ask people about things to do with their heart. Most guys give me a wishy-washy answer, so then I'll pry.

Because I've been a sickly person all my life I suppose every-thing has been relative. People feel sorry for me because I can't walk properly or couldn't play footy. I've had some really down days when I am really hurting and then the next day the pain's not so bad and I feel great about that. I laugh a lot. I'm an absolute goose really. You don't hurt when you laugh. There's always some-thing to be sad about but I don't want to be there for long. I believe I'm an optimist without having my head in the clouds.

I've always had a struggle with money and my health. But I also think I'm gifted with my love of being with people. I can barely walk, I'm crooked and I'm happy—I feel good about myself. I've always had somebody beside me. Maybe I'm confident because I'm happy. When I was in hospital I had to give up my job. I had lots of time to think. Because Jenny had just died I wanted to be at home with the kids so I started my own business. I like working from home and having control of my own life. However, I wish I didn't have to work to earn money. I'd much prefer to do some-thing in the voluntary area.

I've now moved in with my partner. She's great. I knew I didn't want a housewife and I didn't want a mother for my kids. I've never felt so relaxed. We allow each other to be ourselves. We support and help each other to feel comfortable where we are. I just feel blessed, and people say, 'How so?'

I'm conscious of every breath. I get joy out of little things and I seriously feel it. I know it sounds trite but I know that the things that give me joy have little to do with money. These days I trust that my life is at just where it is meant to be. If the worst came I would cope with it better than I ever have. So in a strange way it has helped me that all these terrible things have happened because they have also brought lots of positive things into my life.

GROWTH IN ADVERSITY

At midlife most of us can see that our crucial times of personal growth have been at times of adversity. It is possible to have this focus day to day and see any moment of adversity as a time of possible growth. As you become increasingly centred and balanced within your Self you contain within you the resources to work with and learn from this adversity. As we encounter the rapids (fears), our focus on Self and the knowledge that we have the skills to navigate these rapids and learn means we are much less frightened of them when we experience them.

Many have found, as Manny has, that the daily practice of meditation is a key tool for maintaining a sense of balance and happiness, even at times of adversity. Do you have a daily practice of meditation, prayer or contemplation? If not, would you consider attending a course or reading a book to learn about how to bring such a practice into your life? You could use my notes on meditation in Chapter 5 to start such a practice. You might find, as others have before you, that it is the surest way of being able to live life where you 'relish every moment'.

CHAPTER 22

awakening the feminine

No human value or trait is complete in itself. It must be joined with its masculine or feminine 'mate' in a conscious synthesis if we are to have balance and wholeness.

Robert Johnson, *We*

CARL JUNG USED THE concepts of *anima* and *animus* to explain that in every man there is a woman, and in every woman there is a man. Let's look more closely at this idea. When a baby boy is born he gradually learns that because he is a boy he is expected to behave in a certain way. Others also treat him in a certain way because he is a boy. And so he tends to develop a conscious attitude that displays masculine characteristics, and this is his persona. Because of the psyche's need to keep itself in balance, as the young boy develops he pushes down into his unconscious traditional female ways of being. This is what Jung called his anima. Jung also said that there is an archetypal force of femaleness in all men as well.

In the time that Jung was developing his ideas, people's lives were more clearly defined by their gender than they are today. However, it still is the case that through conditioning, boys and girls have external pressures on them to be a certain way. So they will have the tendency to bury in their unconscious characteristics that are seen as undesirable for somebody of their gender.

For a man at midlife, reclaiming repressed parts of himself and creating more balance in his being and his life has much to do with awakening this unconscious feminine within him. In our power-focused society, honouring the feminine is difficult enough for a woman to do. For a man, brought up to believe that because he is male there is a certain way he needs to be, awakening his feminine can be bewildering and challenging, but ultimately a personally liberating time. From my observations and interviews I found that men experienced this awakening in a variety of ways. There was much experimentation and joy as they allowed themselves to honour their feminine and experience life in a way they hadn't before.

The two words, feminine and masculine, are emotionally loaded in our society. I will illustrate this statement with a simple example. Pat, aged 41, is experiencing inner conflict. There is much to be done at work, with deadlines to be met. There is little time to relax with friends and family or to just 'smell the roses'.

We are all androgynous

As you read the above brief description, did you think Pat was male or female? The description could be of either. Men and women have both the psychological feminine and masculine energies within; however, in our Western society these two words have been so identified with gender, it is difficult for us to accept this under-standing. Carl Jung was the first psychologist to say that we are all made up of both the masculine and the feminine. In our minds we equate men with the masculine and women with the feminine, although we are all in fact androgynous.

In the Western world we have been encouraged to think in opposites—good versus evil, truth versus falsehood, black versus white, masculine versus feminine. We have also been conditioned to use argumentative, adversarial ways of thinking. In order to open up our minds to new possibilities, and to be able to live more creatively at midlife, we can benefit by looking at Eastern teachings, such as those of Chinese philosophy. It uses dialogue more in terms of complementary rather than adversarial positioning. It uses the symbol Yang to denote the masculine, active, aggressive and rational and the Yin to denote the feminine, passive, patient, trusting, intuitive and symbolic. Certainly Eastern philosophy has had a huge influence on our world in the past 40 years, although it is still rare to find places or people in the Western world where the feminine and masculine ways of being are integrated. If we are to move through midlife transition it is vital that we all find creative ways of balancing these ways of being within us.

In our world, both men and women have been conditioned to think that the masculine, Yang way is the best way. When we were young our families and schools encouraged us to relate more to masculine values as they taught us to focus on order, achievement of goals, control and rational thinking. With the impact of the feminist movement many women joined men in a work world where the masculine qualities of strength, independence, competition and focused hard work are acknowledged with admiration, prestige and generous salaries. At midlife, both men and women need to step back from these influences and start identifying more with their feminine energy as it assists them to navigate the transition from the first to the second half of life.

A young boy growing up in the 1950s and 1960s was often encouraged to identify solely with the masculine. He developed an outer, conscious attitude that was active, rational, objective, unemotional and more related to mastering his world. This became his persona. Because of the psyche's need to keep itself in balance, as this occurred, his more feminine attitudes were repressed into his unconscious and became part of his shadow. A man with this type of development in the first half of life will arrive at midlife with his feminine energy buried deep inside him. It is through accessing this feminine within his psyche that he will bring about enormous change and balance in himself and his world at midlife.

THE 'RECONCILED MAN'

In discussing the importance of a man awakening to his feminine at midlife I want to make it clear that it is still very important for him to embrace his masculine energy. I am not suggesting he discard one for the other. This might momentarily happen as he first starts embracing his feminine; however, ultimately the goal is for him to be able to integrate and draw on both energies at the same time. This is the way he will create balance in his life.

In her book, *XY: De l'Identite Masculine*, French professor Elisabeth Badinter presents the term 'the reconciled man'. In her work she talks about the old-fashioned 'hard man' and the often found present-day 'soft man', pointing out the importance of both men and women being able to access both these qualities. She uses the term 'reconciled man' to refer to a man who can draw on both of these energies depending on what he perceives the situation requires. We have greater wisdom when we balance these two energies within us, for each is appropriate in different situations, and in many situations both are necessary. For example, there are situations that a man may grasp intuitively using his feminine energy but then have to justify logically by using his masculine energy. There may also be times when he needs to master an aspect of nature, but he can do it in a sensitive way, using his feminine energy, by considering the ecological aspects of the natural environment. It is the conscious use of both the feminine and masculine attitudes that will lead to the wisest decisions.

LIVING WITH SUPPOSED CONTRADICTIONS

At midlife, a man's psyche pushes up from his unconscious previously repressed and hitherto unknown 'feminine' parts of himself. When this happens he will become aware of supposed contradictions about himself. For example, he is strong—however, he is also vulnerable. It is important for a man to notice and acknowledge these contradictions. They are vehicles for enormous personal growth. Learning to integrate these supposed dichotomies within him leads to creative ways of living at midlife.

As we become aware of contradictions in our life we benefit if we can hold the tension between them and work gently with that tension. If we are to move towards individuation we need to accept that we are composites. No longer will we define ourselves by gender or other conditioning from the first half of our life. By reflecting on the opposites within us, noticing them, accepting them, owning them as part of ourself we begin to realise we can live with that tension. In fact, that tension brings much energy and vitality into our life.

I will give a personal example. Opposites that I continue to struggle to integrate within me are 'to be vigilant' and 'to be relaxed' at the same time. This is a tension within me that I have particularly become aware of in the past couple of years. During this time my first book has been published, I have created a new business around my writing, and there have been many other changes going on inside me as well as in my outer world. To be vigilant is a reflection of the masculine within me, while to be relaxed is a reflection of the feminine within me. I want to be able to do my work and lead my life in a manner that ensures I remain alert to new ways of doing things. At the same time I want to be relaxed in my being.

Create a dialogue between contradictions within you

A tool I have used to explore how I can hold these two supposed opposites within me has been to create a dialogue between them. I often use this 'dialogue exercise' when writing in my journal as I become aware of opposites within me that are causing confusion. When you are first introduced to this concept, it may seem over the top, but remember it is only a tool to help you understand yourself.

It's a bit like a therapy session without the therapist. I use initials to show which part of me is talking. For example, in this case I use RS for my 'relaxed self' and VS for my 'vigilant self'. Here is an example of some dialogue from my journal.

VS: I don't want to miss any of the things I need to notice and do to make sure my work around 'navigating midlife' goes well.

RS: Yes I know, but I feel as though you are always on alert and I often get forgotten.

VS: I don't forget you. I take time off and give you space to just be. Isn't that enough?

RS: Well, I suppose that is true. However, I want to work with you. I want to find a way that we can both be there at the same time. Isn't it possible to be vigilant and relaxed at the same time?

And once I have written the dialogue I realise that this is what I want, and that this is what I am internally struggling with. I don't want to lead a life where I have to stop being vigilant to relax, or vice versa. I want to remain vigilant to my surroundings and to what is inside me, while at the same time relax in my being. I am not assuming I can create this change overnight but by having an ongoing dialogue between these contrasting parts of myself I am hopeful I will slowly move towards integrating them.

When you find supposed opposites in your life you might also find it useful to let them have a dialogue with each other. The idea is that one doesn't have to win over the other. Rather, allow them to communicate with each other, each in turn speaking while the other listens, for there is much personal insight and vitality to be gained at midlife if we can hold the tension of opposites within us. Can you think of any opposites within you at the moment that might benefit from having a dialogue with each other?

How conscious are you of the masculine and feminine energies within you? How do you express these different parts of you in the way you lead your life? It is difficult enough for women in the

Western world to integrate the feminine way of being into their lives as societal forces encourage them to remain strong, focused, goal-oriented and rational. For a man, especially of the baby boomer generation, it can seem like a daunting undertaking. At midlife, however, he has the support of his psyche as it encourages him to access this important part of himself.

IT IS NOT ABOUT OUTER APPEARANCE

From my interviews and observations I found that this awakening of the feminine in a man may at first express itself in more outer signs. He may desire to dress differently—be more flamboyant, wear more colour. One of my interviewees experimented with wearing women's underwear for a day. However, bringing the feminine into his life isn't about what a man wears. This is just an outer manifestation of an inner need. This is not to say that a man might not rightfully change the way he dresses. Men's clothing in the Western world, especially in the business world, has been so 'grey', predictable and unimaginative; it can be very liberating for a man at midlife to give himself the freedom to explore different ways of dressing.

There is much trial and error and ongoing vigilance required if a man is to bring more of the feminine into his life. Honouring his feminine is not about wearing a floral shirt or growing long hair. It's about allowing himself to let go, to stop trying to control both people and situations, and to trust in fate and the natural rhythm of life. It's about noticing himself as he moves through his day and creating a life that nurtures his being. It's about being in contact with his own emotional world and being able to share this world with others.

From my interviews I found that there were a variety of ways men experienced their first awakening of the feminine. A life-changing experience for Robert was when he was having a massage at 39 years of age. He described how when the masseur said to him, 'Imagine there's a tiny ball of golden light in your heart', he started to cry and didn't stop for two days. He said that after this his world changed irrevocably. He felt that his body physically softened and he had a sensitivity for himself and others, which until then he had never been conscious of. Simon described how once he started a daily practice of meditation, after a life-threatening illness, he created time to nurture himself as well as time to spend with his three sons. After separating, Gary started to nurture himself, realising there was nobody there anymore to do this for him. First he learnt how to cook, and then as a way of controlling his stress levels he started to run a bath for himself in the evening, using essential oils, playing relaxing classical music and making sure he put the answering machine on so he couldn't be interrupted. He attended art classes after finally accepting what his inner voice had been telling him to do for many years. As he started his first class he said he felt an extra-ordinary shift inside him. He felt a release of emotion and with it an ease and acceptance of himself that he had never felt before.

CREATING TIME TO AWAKEN YOUR FEMININE

These men are all talking about changes brought about as they awoke the feminine within. You might like to consider how you could consciously create time to awaken your feminine. Do you ever give time to just be with yourself? Would you consider spending time sitting in the sun while reading, soaking up the sound of the birds and the wind in the trees; or writing in a journal; or listening to your favourite music while lying on a couch; or dancing around the room; or taking a bath with essential oils? What are you willing to create in your life right now to help you embrace your feminine? Whatever you decide to do to create some time to honour your feminine, I suggest you have no deadlines, no clear structure and no 'shoulds' or 'musts'. And as you learn to do this for just a moment, an hour, or perhaps a whole day, you will gradually learn how to awaken the feminine within you so that it is there with you for the rest of your life.

CHAPTER 23

embracing your
inner child

. . . the need to find the inner child is part of
every human being's journey towards wholeness.

John Bradshaw, *Healing the Shame That Binds You*

THE CONCEPT OF THE 'inner child' seemed pretty whacky to me
up to a couple of years ago. I suppose I had done little to understand
how others used it. I now understand that as adults we all have our
inner child inside us; the child that was brought into the world when
we were born. As we find ways at midlife to reconnect with this inner
child we bring much of the energy and way of being that come with
it. Being in contact with our inner child brings vitality and joy into
our life, along with a desire to explore different ways of living in the
second half of our life. Let me explain further why our inner child is
so important.

YOU WERE BORN A WONDER CHILD

Each of us was born a wonder child. We were born innocent, naive,
joyous, playful and with a sense of wonder about the world around
us. As we moved through childhood we collected wounds, to varying

degrees depending on our childhood circumstances. Perhaps you had a parent who never listened to you, or always said that you were dumb, or that the world wasn't safe, or who actually acted in an abusive way so that you didn't feel safe. Or perhaps they wanted you to be a very different boy to the one you felt you were underneath. As a child you were vulnerable and powerless. You accepted that your parents and other 'wise' adults knew better than you. You believed that what they said or did was the way the world actually was. To control your fears of abandonment, rejection, humiliation and shame you curtailed your behaviour so as to make yourself safe. By degrees your 'wounded child' replaced your 'wonder child'.

When people undertake psychoanalysis they will spend many years exploring their childhood to dig out all their wounds. In some ways this is what I did when I went to counselling over a period of several years in my early forties, although it certainly wasn't as extensive or as expensive an experience as psychoanalysis. Consulting a well-qualified professional can be useful when we want to understand more about our childhood wounds and how they are limiting the way we are presently living our life. I also believe there is much we can do for ourselves, especially after benefiting from outside support through therapy, by observing ourselves, noticing our fears, and being willing to do the inner and outer work. We can contact the emotions and beliefs that created the wounded child, find ways of letting them go, and in the process start reclaiming our wonder child.

As an adult you are not powerless, unless you allow yourself to be so. The world does not have to be as it was when you were a child—you can now make conscious choices to find new ways of responding.

FIND WAYS TO HEAL THE WOUNDS FROM CHILDHOOD

At midlife it is important to revisit your childhood and to reconnect with the wounds from your past. However, this developing awareness is just the first step. You then need to find a way to heal yourself from this past wounding. The pain of your wounded child is what keeps you locked into any compulsive, addictive behaviours. As this pain is coming up from our unconscious at midlife, we can find it so unbearable that we keep our self busy so as to distract our self from the pain. Those who were severely abused as children have more pain and that is why they can be more prone to addiction.

As you heal your wounded child you free yourself of those limiting behaviours that hinder the process of creating a life that reflects who you truly are. Each time you experienced a wounding as a young child, emotional energy got blocked inside you. At midlife your psyche is encouraging you to heal these energy blocks. Your psyche speaks to you, perhaps through your dreams, daydreams, drawings and writing or as an inner voice. At midlife you become more vital as you reconnect with your wounded child and release these emotions that are locked in your body.

CONTACTING YOUR INNER CHILD

In *Healing the Shame That Binds You*, John Bradshaw discusses several steps you can take to reconnect with the wounded child within you and release blocked emotions. First, he suggests you find a way to validate the trauma of the childhood experience. For example, when you tell your story to another, they might say, 'You must have felt really abandoned when your mother left you for two weeks with no explanation'. This might be enough for you to realise it is okay that you felt abandoned as a child when this happened. Perhaps you have never even contemplated this before.

Second, he suggests you need to contact the grief felt around this abandonment. It helps to have another person support you in your grief. So often, when we were young we were made to feel it was wrong to cry and express our grief. This is very damaging to a young child's emotional development. It is important for you to now learn that it is normal to feel and express grief, and to learn to be able to do it in front of another. It is very healing to do so and it is not an intellectual exercise. We actually have to experience the gut-wrenching feelings of grief. Third, Bradshaw suggests you can do something to demonstrate how you would have liked to be treated at the time. For example, write a letter to your parents, which you do NOT send, explaining to them what you needed as a child back then. Or write a letter to your inner child from your parents saying what they wish they had given to you. Fourth, you can meditate on your inner child. In his book John Bradshaw has an inner child meditation you could put on tape, then listen to and make contact with your 'little boy'. I have found that another way of meditating on my 'little girl' after connecting with and working through old wounding from childhood is to lie in bed and hold my 'little girl'. This has been very healing. I have also found a teddy bear comes in handy here. In my early forties a friend and I gave each other a teddy bear. In many ways I initiated the exchange and at the time I observed myself thinking this was very strange behaviour for a woman of my age. Several times I have taken my teddy to bed to hug. And I now realise I was hugging my 'little girl'.

Finally, you can find appropriate ways, now as an adult, to get some of your childhood developmental needs met. Brian, one of the men I interviewed, found that attending a men's group did this for him. I discuss men's groups further in chapter 28. In his men's group Brian has found a place to be 're-fathered' and to learn the male bonding skills a son would ideally learn from his father. Recently I have found it useful to write a dialogue between me and my 'little girl' at times of unease. Here is an example from my journal:

> Have had a pinching feeling in my stomach since Thursday. Was feeling great on Wednesday, but now I feel tired and a little foggy-headed. I realise I need to speak to my little girl. When I neglect her, when I don't look after her, she grabs my attention by becoming emotional—mostly sad—and also I get this tightness down low in my gut. When I looked at her today I could see her as gentle,

loving, affectionate, bewildered and also sad. Perhaps if I have a dialogue with her I can understand how best to look after her.

Me: What can I do for you?
LG: Get to know me. Spend some time with me.
Me: How?
LG: Like this. But also just as you move through your day. Notice me. Give me attention even when I'm not asking for it. Just sense that I am there.
Me: When am I most likely to neglect you?
LG: Much of the time—in fact all of the time—but it is worst when you put pressure on yourself and you don't take time out for play, to be in a place of wonder, no deadlines, just being. Don't give me a hard time when I am tired, or sad, or even playful—just accept me as I am. Perhaps even learn to put aside time for me often— such as at least a couple of hours a week. But in many ways you give me more than that. I love dancing, singing, drawing, being outside, skipping, snuggling up in bed—so we do have time together. But when we are doing these things perhaps just talk to me a little—I'd like that.

As I was reading the typed copy of Michael's interview in which he talks about the turning points in the first half of his life (chapter 11) I became eager to ask him how he had made contact with and healed his wounded 'little boy' from the trauma he experienced at one and a half years of age. I'll repeat the part of his interview I was particularly thinking of.

At one and a half I had an accident which shaped my life profoundly. My face was burned. It happened when I was home with grandma. She was preparing the traditional Sunday lunch while my parents were at church. She was lifting the roast pan and the boiling gravy spilt over my head when the handle slipped. I was in hospital struggling with my life for a few weeks because of blood poisoning following the accident and of course because I was only a year and a half old, that was in my unconscious memory. It is only in the last ten years that I have dug a bit more into my childhood, and have realised how deep an impact that event had in my life. Feeling abandoned by my parents, being in a hospital with my hands and feet tied down because otherwise I would scratch my terribly burned face. And I think the adults lied to me and said I would be home tomorrow, I would be out soon and so on and so that left a deep mark on me.

Michael was only one and a half years old when he was burnt. These memories had been locked away for many years. They would have been deeply buried in his unconscious. How did Michael gain access to these memories? How did he connect to this fear of being abandoned? Several weeks later I found the opportunity to ask him. This is what he told me.

Michael

I remember the moment vividly. It was a cold, rainy, winter's day at the community I was living in. We had planned a gardening day but it was too wet so we just sat around all day drinking coffee and talking about our past. I started talking about the accident. I'd never talked about it before. It hadn't seemed like an important part of my life. As I talked about it I noticed there was a lot of energy in it for me. It wasn't just like recalling a story. I felt strong emotions around it. This surprised me. And then somebody asked 'How has this affected you?'

In the following days I wrote in my journal what I remembered about it and it suddenly appeared to me that it was a very significant event in my life and in a way I had carried it with me. I wrote about it. I talked about it with others. At the same time I lost interest in masturbating, something that had been a big part of my life. This was an indication to me that the remembering had shifted something deep inside me. Then over the months and years

I just started noticing a little boy inside me eager to release these painful experiences. I'd just sit, not being afraid of the pain, and feel it. Feeling the pain of a little boy tied down in a bed because he was so badly burnt. Feelings of being abandoned by his parents. So I connected to the pain without wallowing in it.

Six months later I started counselling training and this gave me the opportunity to continue to explore it with the support of the other trainees. And over the years I realised how profoundly and intrinsically this accident, which I had forgotten as an adult, has shaped my life. When I lose the little boy I feel anxious, pressured, alone, abandoned, grey, dull, with fear of failure and no joy in my life—just plodding along. When I notice this I acknowledge I have lost communication with him because old fears are emerging. Then I go looking for him and talk to him about what he is fearful of.

I now know I can only be present to the extent I am in touch with my little boy. I cannot live in the now with the little boy in hiding. To open my heart, to connect with the world, to smell the roses—it is only possible to the degree that I am at peace with my inner child.

THE WOUNDED CHILD IS ALSO THE WONDER CHILD

There are many benefits in contacting your inner child, especially at midlife. As you make time to notice and care for your wounded child, you bring all the joy of your wonder child into your life at the same time. What do you need to do to make time for your 'little boy'? What wounds might he have that need healing? What might he enjoy?

PART 6

Outer support helps you navigate

CHAPTER 24

support on your
journey

*The spiritual awakening that is taking place counter culturally will
become more of a daily norm as we willingly break mainstream cultural
taboos that silence or erase our passion for spiritual practice.*

H. Bell, *All About Love*

OUR WESTERN CULTURE has few, if any, commonly accepted
understandings to acknowledge that the second half of life is a time
for spiritual awakening. Understandings about this time of spiritual
awakening are portrayed in our music, poetry, songs, art and writing
although until our attention is drawn to them we remain oblivious
to them. In contrast, in countries such as India there are rituals,
traditions and understandings that acknowledge midlife is a time to
start immersing oneself in a spiritual life. Hinduism divides the life
cycle into quarters—student, householder, hermit and renunciant—
each quarter representing a period of 25 years. Western culture
only considers development to the 'householder stage' and then
in many ways pronounces it a downhill slide from there on as the
body physically declines. In their book, *Wisdom of the Elders*, Peter
Knudtson and David Suzuki point out that the Native Mind (as

represented by such cultures as the North American Indians and Aboriginal Australians) 'tends to honour as its most esteemed elders those individuals who have experienced a profound and compassionate reconciliation of outer and inner directed knowledge, rather than virtually anyone who has made material achievement or simply survived to chronological old age'. This 'reconciliation of outer and inner directed knowledge' is achieved as we move through midlife transition.

As our Western culture denies the importance of this spiritual awakening at midlife, it forgoes the important contribution and role that wise elders play in a healthy society. Much guidance and wisdom can come from a person who has done the personal work to move towards wholeness. We suffer both individually and as a society as long as our Western culture remains stuck in the householder stage with its limited focus on outer, material ideals.

Denial of the importance of the spiritual aspect of life means there are societal forces that can discourage us from going on this journey. We need to become conscious of barriers to our spiritual development at midlife and develop practices to counteract them. These practices allow us to nurture and care for our own spiritual life, and in so doing contribute to the nurture and care of the spiritual life of our society, and ultimately of our world.

RECONNECT WITH YOUR QUESTIONING, CURIOUS SELF

Many of us have to reclaim the questioning, curious parts of our nature if we are to move beyond societal forces that can limit our spiritual development. Anybody who has been a parent or who has worked with young children knows that children are immensely curious and open to the wonder and mystery of life. For many of us born in the 1950s and 1960s this questioning, curious nature was repressed as we conformed to the many pre-existing rules that were part of our childhood.

I will share with you an example from my own childhood to show you what I mean. I went to a girls' church school from just four years of age and remained there until the end of my school days, just after my seventeenth birthday. From the beginning the discipline at school was very strict. There were many rules, many of which I didn't understand. Very quickly I learnt that if you questioned you got into trouble, so much of the time I tried to be quiet and not question— the direct opposite of my true nature. Sometimes my natural vitality and curiosity broke through, often with dire consequences. So rather than being encouraged to be open, curious and questioning, we were conditioned to be passive. School was also a place of memorisation. For example, our classwork consisted of memorising long passages by heart, and then rewriting them from memory. Throughout my schooling there was little room for me to exercise my mind or to find my own meaning in what I was reading and listening to. I learnt that my own thoughts, ideas and understandings were not important to the adults around me. Consequently, I also learnt not to value or trust them myself.

My experiences at the local Sunday school were similar. I vividly remember one Sunday morning when I was twelve years old. In trying to grapple with the teacher's interpretation of the lesson I asked a question: 'Do you mean to say that because I was born here and happen to be a Christian, rather than being born in some other country like India or China where I might practise another religion, I am a better person? Surely no matter where I live or no matter what I believe, I am the same being.' The teacher leant over and hit me on the arm. That was the end of the discussion.

I recount these events as I believe it was childhood experiences like these that gradually eroded the open, questioning, curious nature I was born with. I learnt not to question or challenge what I observed around me. I became outwardly passive in many aspects of my life. Inside I was still questioning, although often at a barely conscious level and rarely expressed. It wasn't until I started to meditate in my mid-thirties that my curious, questioning self started to reawaken.

It wasn't for several years that I fully began to trust this part of myself. Gradually my heart and mind opened and I began to seek answers to a myriad of questions. And once this quest began, it became a vital part of my spiritual awakening as I reconnected with the inborn questioning and curious parts of my self.

LEARN TO QUESTION THE 'STATUS QUO'

While carrying out research for my writing it has become clear to me that there are many forces discouraging men and women from going on this journey of transformation at midlife. For example, for women, there is such a focus on our hormonal changes at midlife that our important psychological and spiritual development at this time of life may be completely overlooked. As an example of how strong this mindset is for women, when my first book *Navigating Midlife: women becoming themselves* was sent out to the media, my publisher had to include in the package a red sheet of paper on which was written in large black letters, 'This is not a book about menopause'.

Many women at midlife are prescribed antidepressants or hormone replacement therapy for their ongoing turbulent feelings. Several women I know have been told by their general practitioner that they may need to be on antidepressants for the rest of their life. From my observation the one thing these women have in common is a strong life force. Could it be that these women, sensing a desire for change at midlife, have strong feelings about doing so, which if repressed lead to depression? As they continue to experience forces discouraging them from honouring these feelings and creating the changes necessary to honour themselves, they experience ongoing depression. The denial of the importance of these feelings as an indication of a need for change only compounds the problem. I will take an example from my own life to explain what I mean.

MY EARLY MIDLIFE EXPERIENCE

As I started to meditate and connect with my inner world at midlife I experienced emotional turmoil and health problems as I felt the incongruence between the person I was beginning to understand I was, and the life I was living. I was angry, depressed and lethargic with swinging energy levels, increasing muscle tension and gynaecological problems. I was bewildered. What was happening to me? I didn't have the understandings I now have about midlife. Was I going crazy? There were continual visits to my doctor who referred me on to a series of specialists to try to diagnose my physical and emotional changes. A gynaecologist suggested I take hormone replacement therapy; however, with my mother's history of breast cancer in her early forties I knew this was not wise. I was then referred to a psychiatrist who prescribed antidepressants which numbed all my feelings while the concurrent counselling encouraged me to 'fit in' to my present lifestyle. Then I was referred to a psychologist in whom I had no confidence, but I felt too desperate to stop going.

On the surface all looked fine. I was married to a hardworking man, had three healthy children, was financially secure, had a lovely home and a career as a psychologist. What could I possibly have to complain about? Finally it all came to a head on my fortieth birthday. I remember walking down the passage and into the dining room where the well-wishers were. I was numb with despair. I was dumb with terror. Did they notice? I attempted a smile. I moved through the room. I was a skin with nothing inside. I had to keep going through the motions. I couldn't let anybody know. Could they see my emptiness? Could they feel my emptiness? Could I keep it up? How long to go? By luck, the next day I was referred to a health professional who helped me to start accepting my feelings of anger, sadness and lethargy and my desire for change. Soon my health problems disappeared.

I recount my early midlife story here to demonstrate how, at first, when we start to experience the turbulent feelings and desire for change that so often mark the beginnings of midlife transition, we may be sent messages that encourage us to see it as a physical problem rather than as a time of psychological and spiritual growth. Recently a female client described how her husband's doctor had sent him off for physical tests, including hormonal analysis. From her description of his symptoms it seems clear to me that he is experiencing changes typical for a man in the beginning stages of midlife transition. So it seems that now a man may also be prescribed hormone treatment at midlife. And although it is not common for men to be told it is 'just hormonal' there are many other societal forces that discourage them from going on this journey. For example, if a man visits his GP with mood swings he is likely to be prescribed antidepressants. Antidepressants may be of use; however, unless they are accompanied by appropriate counselling, they may block his ongoing development.

We can also be discouraged by colleagues, friends and family from making the changes we need to make if we are to honour our own psychological and spiritual development at midlife. As a man wishes to cut down on his working hours to make more time for himself, or a woman decides to make some time for herself at the expense of meeting others' needs, they can easily experience strong resistance from those around them. For example, Mark, a medical specialist in his early forties, described to me that when he decided to not work late into the evenings so as to spend them with his wife and young children, he experienced much ridicule and jibing from his colleagues.

SEEK OUT APPROPRIATE SUPPORT

There was little, if anything in my training as a psychologist about the significance of midlife transition, and I believe it is the same for other health professionals. If you consult a health professional, bear in mind that they may have little understanding about the significance of midlife transition.

We have to search carefully for appropriate support at midlife. What support do you have in your life to assist you as you journey midlife transition? Do you have friends and family that will support you to make the changes that are inevitable on this journey? Do you have others you can speak to about the feelings and thoughts inside you? If you wanted to learn to meditate, write, do photography, draw or sing, would you know how to go about seeking a course to do these? How could you develop the resourceful part of your nature? What self-sabotaging talk might be stopping you? Books have been an immense support to me at midlife. Do you ever take the time to browse in a bookshop or your local library? I find that in this browsing I am often led to exactly the book I need for my ongoing spiritual journey. Who or what are you willing to bring into your life to support you on this journey? The next chapters offer some suggestions for seeking out the support of others as you navigate midlife transition.

CHAPTER 25

counselling

The calls have come from men across the socio-economic spectrum.
The main issues they want to discuss relate to family breakdown,
social isolation and relationship, work or sexual issues.

Mensline manager Terry Melvin, quoted in
The Australian Financial Review, 11 April 2002, discussing the
huge response from distressed men to their telephone service for men

I REMEMBER A conversation I had with a man I was sitting next to at a dinner. It was about fifteen years ago. He would have been in his mid-forties. Towards the end of the dinner he explained that he had just left his third marriage. I asked, 'Did you ever go to counselling?' and he replied, 'Oh no, I couldn't do that. I'd feel like such a failure.'

Men are often so conditioned to think of themselves as strong and self-reliant that it can be a huge step for them to seek out support through counselling. The high usage of telephone counselling for men, such as through Mensline, has shown there is a huge need by men for this kind of support. Mensline manager, Terry Melvin, is quoted in *The Australian Financial Review* as saying:

We don't adhere to a strict counselling model but tend to be
fairly laid-back and take a conversation talk approach. We

chat and try to be pragmatic, moving towards solutions. Men don't just want to ventilate their problems. They want strategies to manage them. That said, however, once we engage, there is usually no problem getting to the deep grief, loss and hurt that often underpins their experience.

It is not such a big step for a man to pick up the phone and talk at a time of need as it is to make an appointment and physically commit to fronting up to another person to share vulnerabilities. In this chapter I share how one of my interviewees came to counselling and his experience of it.

JOHN

John's attitude to his experience of counselling is typical. At first he was reluctant to go; however, once there, he derived great benefit from it. To put John's experience of counselling into some context, I will first let you get to know a little about him as I recall some of our interview. As you read, do you relate to any of his life experiences? Have you ever sought out counselling? If you thought it might help you, would anything stop you from going?

John: I had a trouble-free adolescence. I enjoyed school. There was no trauma. I didn't really notice adolescence—it just happened. After leaving school at 18 I went through some changes, learning how to deal with things outside the comfortable confines of school and family, meeting members of the opposite sex in a concerted way and continuing to work out who I was. And at 27 I married and from that time on there were two strands to my life—my professional life and my marriage and family life—both of which have had a profound influence on how I have been in my middle years.

From the beginning I felt I needed to work hard as I was the type of person who contributes to things and makes them better than I find them. Also I was ambitious. I have a very competitive streak in me and I wanted to be recognised as the best. Consequently, I've worked very hard in my career. This has had consequences on the other side of my life. I always envisaged I'd have a family and be part of the family scene and so I got married and it was a pretty mixed experience for me, and ended badly in divorce in my late forties. It started ending badly several years before that, and there were profoundly miserable times. I felt unvalued and my whole sense of self-worth was undermined and it left me with a yawning need for affirmation, appreciation, recognition and love. On reflection, I've become a very needy person in midlife, whereas earlier I always saw myself as self-reliant, somebody who could satisfy my own needs.

Part of the reason for the collapse of my marriage was because I worked too hard and didn't pay enough attention to it. And also being emotionally closed as a consequence of coming from an all-boy family and going to an all-boys' school. You had to close yourself off for self-preservation—it's certainly not good for learning about emotions.

So, if I look at the changes I experienced in my forties, it was the loss of a sense of self-worth in those last years of my marriage. This was the first defining change of how I experienced midlife. And there was a yawning chasm of need and it probably wasn't as big a change as I thought it was at the time. I don't think anything changed that much. I just noticed things and the impact of external events on me changed. I felt things differently. In retrospect, if I look back at this period of life, I was probably seriously depressed.

Robyn: What makes you say that?

John: I've had periods of deep gloom since the end of my marriage— I've had that clinically verified—I've fought my way out of it. I now recognise the feeling. It made things add up to me—as to how things had been towards the end of my marriage.

Since being separated and then divorced I suppose the midlife years have been ones where I've spent a lot of energy to find myself again. At 53 I think I've arrived at a pretty good point. I can again stand on my own two feet—and I can give. I'm feeling strong and I have a feeling that I'm okay again after many years of struggling.

Robyn: What have you done to get to this place?

John: To some degree it was trying to find reasons to feel good about myself. Redefining myself—that as an individual I'm a worthwhile human being and that I have things to offer other people.

Robyn: Did anything specifically help you to do this?

John: I went to counselling for a year and a half. I visited my GP as I was feeling so bad. He recommended counselling and after some hesitation I decided to go.

Robyn: Could you tell me a little bit about it?

John: It was quite frightening at first because I had to bare parts of my soul that were very painful. I had to go back and identify the lack in my life, people not viewing me as worthwhile. I began to understand, under grilling by the counsellor, that I hadn't ever experienced unconditional love. The expectations that had already existed around my family were conditions. I also had to come to grips with the fact that I had never felt loved in my marriage. I found all of this very depressing and sad and I was confronted with the fact that I'd been very depleted by the experience—my whole life had depleted me and I needed to find some sort of strength. And as I talked to the counsellor he was very affirming of me and I found it a great source of strength that he thought I was a warm person with very good people skills—I think my people skills had got better during the past couple of years. The counsellor said I would be a very good friend to anyone. I'd not felt that for at least five years. I'd been a miserable friend to everyone, including my wife. And the one thing I clung to was to be there for my daughters. In many ways that was the anchor that allowed me to build my sense of self. It was a very dark experience and I clawed myself back to be a relatively healthy person.

And so there have been big changes and I'm still changing to become a more open person—to ensure what I value gets the priority and attention and not get rocked and lose faith in myself. It's a relearning process, as I was really knocked off my feet by the end of my marriage and the view I had of myself. I've struggled not to be so needy.

Robyn: What do you mean by needy?

John: Needing people to affirm that I'm okay because I didn't feel okay about myself. I've always thought it was important. When young I felt I was worthwhile as an individual and I could withstand pressure. This was fundamental. To find in midlife I'd lost that inner strength and needed another person to affirm me was devastating. That's the basic reason I went to counselling. To rediscover what sort of person I was and what I needed to change to regain my sense of self. During that time the counsellor said I was badly depressed. I declined medication and he said it would take a lot longer.

Robyn: Why did you decline medication?

John: I didn't like the idea of mind-altering drugs. Call it primitive conservatism if you like.

Robyn: What are some of the other things you discussed at counselling?

John: My family's expectations. They were set by reference to other family members who had achieved great things. I don't blame anybody for that.

Robyn: How were those expectations made known to you?

John: It was atmospheric rather than verbal. Occasional remarks might be made, not even to me. If my mother knew the impact some of her comments made on me she'd be mortified. I think it left me with an inner feeling I would never have identified by myself, this inner feeling of never having been loved unconditionally. It's an inner feeling and not necessarily true.

Robyn: How have these expectations affected you?

John: I don't know what made me ambitious and made me want to be the best—perhaps that was an influence.

In a sense I've talked about not feeling a sense of worth. My career has been important in giving me one field of my life where I've consistently been praised and recognised as having worth. It's almost monetary worth—but also worth in a broader sense. Therefore throughout the time of emotional struggle at midlife—broken-heartedness—my work has been an important influence and a counterbalance to emotional distress.

Robyn: Have you put more into work at midlife?

John: No. I've put a lot but not more. I've become more savvy. I've made a bigger contribution as I've helped to build the business.

Robyn: Did you work hard before midlife?

John: Yes. I always had ambition and the desire to be number one. I never recognised it at the time. I used to say to myself that I was pretty laid-back and that being the best didn't mean anything to me. But now I realise I felt driven to work hard, to be seen as a contributor. This is something I learnt when young. I have running through my mind, 'Always put in more than you take out'. This was a very strong piece of learning for me.

Robyn: Do you still think it is a useful message?

John: It's had a profound influence on how I see relationships with other people. I don't think it's a useful piece of learning. If restated as, 'Don't freeload', I think that is more useful. If I think, 'Always put in more than you take out', it doesn't seem to work for me or for anyone else. I still work hard, but I now have a life plan to be secure enough to retire in five years' time. I don't mean retire and go to the beach, but to step out of full-time employment. I want to create a decent lifestyle.

Robyn: And so what do you see now as your challenges from day to day?

John: For my life to reflect what I value.

Robyn: And what do you value?

John: First, I want to create more time to see my two daughters. I also enjoy time with my partner. I then want to create more time for myself. I've always liked spending time by myself. I'm a reflective kind of person and the more time I have for that, the happier I am. The less time I have for it, the more rattled I get and I lose my way. My work has robbed me of reflective time and right now as I play a senior executive role in my organisation I have less time for it, when I actually need more. And I also want to make time for other important people in my life. At sixteen when I was asked what I valued most it was my friends. I think I've lost sight of that along the way and I've been inattentive. I've rediscovered how valuable they are—not just valuable, but also what fun I have with them. My daughters also. I've also always derived a lot of benefit, a feeling of wellbeing from physical exercise. So another goal for me is to make time to be more physically active.

Robyn: At 53 you are moving from midlife transition into middle adulthood. Have you any idea of where you would like to lead your second half of life? What it might look like?

John: At the age of 53 I'm feeling myself ending years of terrible emotional struggle. There have been times of great pleasure and my job has given me satisfaction, but by and large it's been a time of struggle. I have a clearer view now of what's important to me. I think I feel more stable, more centred in terms of who I am and how I am. I need to define my goals in life in reference to the things I really value, and then work out what I need to do.

Robyn: But how can you be really sure about what is important in your life?

John: You have to recognise what gives you a buzz, what makes you happy, and if you are ambitious you need to recognise that.

Robyn: Stephen Covey talks about often when we are ambitious we can be so busy trying to climb the ladder, we forget to notice that it is actually leaning on the wrong wall. Do you think that analogy relates to your experience at all?

John: His life is impossibly perfect. You need to allow for imperfection. I think the wrong-walling I did was to not realise I also had to skill myself for success in my personal life. If you are as unskilled as I was in communicating around emotional issues—and you value your family life—you need to do something there beyond just being yourself. You need to learn new skills. In my professional life I have always recognised the need to learn new skills—in my personal life I hadn't realised there was the same need. I now realise we continually need to re-tool ourselves depending on what we want out of life. The same self isn't necessarily going to be able to achieve your goals. Stephen Covey also says that the most precious resource we have is time. It's allocation of my time I think will bring about either the achievement of my goals, attainment of my values—or the opposite, failure. So that is what I am going to concentrate on.

COUNSELLING CAN ADDRESS YOUR NEEDS — AND YOUR DREAMS

The main focus for this chapter is to encourage you to consider whether you would benefit from counselling, as there are a variety of reasons why it can be useful at midlife. It can offer you a safe and supportive place to explore feelings and thoughts about yourself and your world. You might seek out counselling because of a specific need or just a general feeling that your life could be more fulfilling.

John's interview also raises another issue that affects many men. A lot of boys growing up in the 1950s and 1960s were greatly affected by societal expectations. Their mother's limited psychological development also often greatly affected them. Before the feminist movement most women had little opportunity to express and develop their masculine side as they matured. However, once they had given birth to a son they had the perfect person to carry their 'animus' for them. At midlife this is a heavy burden for a man to carry as it leads to him putting a huge amount of his life and his time into pursuing his mother's dreams, rather than his own. In his interview John explained that it was while having counselling at midlife that he acknowledged for the first time how ambitious he was. He also acknowledged the impact his mother's comments had on him over the years. It can be a huge step for a man to acknowledge and inevitably grieve over how much of his life has unconsciously been spent trying to fulfil another's dreams. Take a moment now to reflect on these questions:

- Are you fulfilling your parents' or another's dreams, rather than your own?
- If you created a life shaped around your own dreams what would it look like?
- Would you consider going to counselling if you knew it might help you to realise your own dreams?
- If not, would you consider picking up the phone and dialling a telephone counselling service such as Mensline?

workshops, seminars and courses

Successful ageing means giving to others joyously whenever one is able, receiving from others gratefully whenever one needs it, and being greedy enough to develop one's own self in between.

G. Vaillant, *Ageing Well: Surprising Guideposts to a Happier Life from the Harvard Study of Adult Development*

MEN I INTERVIEWED have attended seminars, courses and workshops on personal development, tai chi, sound work, singing, drama, dance, creative writing, art, massage, photography, cooking and yoga. Attending seminars, workshops and courses is an easy and enjoyable way to discover more about who we are and what can bring energy and passion into our being at midlife. Yet, nearly always there are significantly more women than men present. Why is it that so few men participate in these types of activities? It is the same whether the facilitator is a man or a woman, so it is not for that reason. Men can enjoy these activities, and others, just as much as women, so I don't believe it is for that reason either. Would you attend a seminar, workshop or series of classes to explore a possible new interest, to explore your self or to just bring more enjoyment and aliveness into your being? One of my interviewees attended a life-changing seminar. As you read about some of his experiences there you might like to try some of the exercises he found so useful.

Richard: A turning point for me was when I attended a weekend seminar. I had just turned 41. Looking back now I can see that I shook off a whole lot of self-limiting beliefs while there.

Robyn: What made you go to the seminar?

Richard: A client cum friend suggested it. She'd been trying to get me there for two years. She sensed I wasn't totally satisfied and didn't know where to go. From a business point of view some of my partners wanted to grow the business, whereas I wanted to look at lifestyle issues. I also realised that some of them didn't know how to manage people. At the same time as I was acknowledging that I wasn't happy, one of my close friends became seriously ill. When my client/friend asked me again to attend the seminar, I did some soul-searching and realised I had a huge fear of committing myself to myself. I talked this over with her and finally decided to go.

Robyn: What was the focus of the seminar?

Richard: Being centred on yourself, about balance, and the importance of listening to your inner voice. I came away feeling empowered to say no and to take control of where I want to go; for me to set my own path, instead of others setting it for me.

On the second day they got us to do an exercise in fifteen minutes. You had to pick out five fears you've acknowledged but been unable to let go of. I picked:

- fear of rejection
- fear of failure
- fear of losing a loved one
- fear of losing myself too much in alcohol
- fear of lack of spirit in my life.

We then did a meditation and visualisation exercise and were encouraged to let these fears go. I got rid of a lot of pain inside me.

I howled a lot about my mother's death and also a friend's death from when I was young. During that time we were actually locked in for the hour. So nobody was allowed to leave. This released a huge amount of momentum in me. Now when something confronts me I don't wallow, I just move on. I also listen to my own inner voice a lot, and when at the gym I say things to myself like:

- I'm a great father
- I'm a great businessman
- I love life
- I'm in control.

I also say them to myself out loud while running around the park.

I now say to friends, 'It's everyone's choice to go for what they want'. It's helped me. It's freed me up but I still feel as though I have a long way to go. I still feel sad about my mother's and my friend's death. From a relationship point of view I feel quite adequate, but because of these losses I am a little wary. I also know I want to bring more spirit into my life, although even as I say it, I am not exactly sure what I mean. I just know there is something more—it's hard to explain.

I also feel as though I did release a bit of fear around failure. I'll back myself in certain things, I'll stand up for myself more. The way I run meetings now, I have a lot more control—but I do feel as though I want to keep moving forward.

Momentum has become my favourite word. Since I went to the seminar seven months ago I've taken real control of our sales team and we're up 60 per cent.

Robyn: What do you mean by your sales team?
Richard: It's my team. If somebody has an issue they come to me. At the same time I have also got in a consultant to the business and she has been like a mentor and a coach for me. I now have more confidence in putting into place changes I have wanted to make for a

long time. She's given me unconditional commitment of support. When I have that type of support I tend to thrive. Having a coach gives me confidence to do things. I really think she has made a huge difference to me, and has helped me follow through on many of the work issues I knew I wanted to tackle as a result of the insights I had at the seminar. She also gives me books to read and she's really supported me in thinking about how I structure my day.

Robyn: Can you tell me a little about a typical day?

Richard: I get up at six and either do some exercise and say affirmations as I do, or I sit in a chair and reflect. I take every second Friday off. For example, this morning I took my daughter to school, went to the gym where I feel as though I am 'putting muscle back in to my life', and then I took my youngest son to the park for a kick of the footy. I then had a shower, a shave and lunch, and then sat in a chair to reflect before I came here. I've taken a lot more control of my time. It's more structured. There are zoned times for the family. I also have to have time for myself otherwise I don't have the focus I want.

In my work there are six hours that are non-negotiable. Things like meeting with my sales team. Outside that time I have flexibility and because my management style is more coaching than actually doing, I have more free time. I'm focusing on building the people. It's more effective. I'm adding value to the business and I enjoy it. I'm also making time for my children to see me work. Last month I took my daughter out with me while I worked on a Saturday. I gave her a few small things to do and she acted as my assistant and then we went and had lunch together and I told her a bit about my work. I'm now quite conscious of having that kind of contact with my children. I pick them up from their activities. This helps me to feel centred and balanced.

At the seminar we were also asked to write down in five minutes what we were really passionate about. For me it was music, family, swimming, reading and the beach. We were then asked what we really hated. For me it was possessiveness. Then we were asked to do a visualisation exercise: Imagine you are older and you are looking back on your life. What is most important? To me, family stood out. And also having a sense that I had my own business. And I feel as though I have now truly committed to both. I make conscious, non-negotiable time for my family and I've now bought in, in a psychological way, to the business. I've now accepted it is mine along with others. I'm no longer sitting on the fence.

At times there is conflict between my work and home. Sometimes something unexpectedly comes up at work, which means I can't honour a family commitment. Whereas before I would feel awful, now I just say to Jan, 'You can tell me I'm a bastard, I'm the worst husband in the world, but it won't hurt me.'

Because of my personality I was always wanting to please. Now I'm not like that—I say a lot more of what I think. I'm much more open. I feel more committed to my marriage. I think my wife gets a bit bewildered at times, though, with all the changes in me.

Exploring new understandings and interests

Seminars, workshops and courses can be an effective way to open up to new understandings about our Self and what we might want to bring into our life as a way of expressing this new understanding. Some seminars and workshops, such as the one Richard attended, are more focused on Self awareness-raising than on exploration of new interests. These Self awareness-raising seminars and workshops can be very worthwhile; however, they need to be approached with some caution, especially if there are large numbers present. When we first open up to our inner, emotional world at midlife it can be quite overwhelming. With many people present there is no opportunity for participants to get the individual attention that may be necessary. If you attend a seminar or workshop where you experience profound changes you might like to consider following it up with some individual support, such as counselling.

To find out about workshops and seminars in your local area you could ring your local council of adult education or a known personal development related institutions and ask them to send you information on their courses. Health-oriented magazines are also a good resource, as well as noticeboards in your local health food shop or community centre. You could also just ask around! You might like to take some time now to ask yourself, 'What interest would I like to explore? How could I bring it into my life?'

Finally deciding to attend a creative writing workshop at my local adult education centre in my mid-forties led me to become a full-time writer and to my vocation for the second half of my life. Up until attending this course I had said to myself all my life, 'I can't write'. Certainly it had always been a dream of mine to be a writer, although I always thought it would have to be in the next life, not this one. Could there equally be a passion, a 'golden' part of you lying dormant? Would you be willing to step out of your comfort zone to explore yourself and your world to discover this gold? What have you got to lose? And imagine what you might gain.

CHAPTER 27

retreats

When we are less goal-directed, we can stand back a little to allow grace, the unplanned and unexpected gift, to enter our lives.

Tim Costello, *Tips from a Travelling Soul Searcher*

DURING MY FORTIES I made time to retreat from my 'normal life' to experience myself in a variety of different settings. When one uses the word 'retreat' some people see it as a time of quiet contemplation, perhaps in a monastery or an ashram. I use the term more broadly in this chapter. For me, a retreat can be any time that I retreat from the 'hurly-burly' of everyday life, to stop attending to all those other things I normally attend to, and give over much of this time to attending to my Self.

I have attended several retreats facilitated by Chris James. He is well known for his innovative work around the healing power of sound. I came across him 'by chance' just after separating from my eighteen-year marriage. My first weekend without my three children was coming up and I decided it was an opportunity to do something for myself. I also thought it would be good for me to have some company. I remembered that acquaintances had organised a weekend residential retreat for the coming weekend. I rang up and booked despite having little idea what it was about. That weekend I started to learn about how to use sound for centring, balancing and healing.

It also led to an increased awareness of how to support my being while public speaking by focusing on how I use my voice and breath, and my posture. Working with Chris also helped me to start moving my energy down into my body, and in many ways to wake it up. This significant journey with sound culminated in my learning from Chris how to teach this sound work to others. I now use sound and breath work in my seminars and retreats to complement my own work as I have found it has been a joyous and effective way of opening up to more of my Self at midlife.

I met Duncan at one of Chris's retreats. As I correctly assumed he was at midlife I asked him if we could meet after the retreat had finished so he could tell me a little bit about his story, including how he had come to be interested in Chris's work and also what aspects he most enjoyed about attending the retreat.

Duncan

I'm 42 years old. I grew up on a small farm in the Mallee and at 17 I enlisted in the army where I trained as an apprentice mechanic. On my weekends I played in the local footy team, spending time with the boys having a drink and otherwise I was quite happy in my own company. I enjoyed my work and the comradeship with the other mechanics in the workshop. About five years ago I became restless and on Sundays would just get into my car and drive. I'd go for walks in the bush, or just go and have a drink somewhere by myself. I was a bit surprised at myself as I hadn't done this sort of thing before.

After a couple of months I was passing through a town where there was a market and I felt a strong pull to stop and have a look. There were all these stalls on things I had never heard about. I was drawn to a stall that had all these beautiful crystals. When I picked up one in particular I felt this tingly feeling in my hands. It fascinated me. There were all sorts of other things there. People were doing tarot readings and giving massage and reiki therapy. It felt easy and welcoming to be there and so I stayed until they started to pack up. Before I left I found out when and where the next market might be.

I continued to visit markets over the next six months and it became the highlight of my life. I couldn't wait until they came around. I didn't talk to the guys at work or to anybody else about what I was doing. I knew they wouldn't understand. I kept bumping into Jenny, she ran the crystal stall, and we would chat. Eventually we just seemed to fall into a relationship together and have been together ever since. I can't believe I have her in my life.

A year after we met, Jenny and I went to the Port Fairy Music Festival with her children, Luke and Kate. All this music—I didn't know how to choose—it was all so good and in many ways I just followed Jenny. It was there that I first saw Chris. On the second afternoon there was this huge number of people, it seemed like several thousand, gathered in front of one of the stages. Jenny wanted to go to another tent. I decided to join the large crowd. Soon this large man—and I don't just mean in size, he had this amazing presence—came onto the stage. When he asked us all to stand in the 'horse position' (feet hip-width apart with toes slightly turned in and knees slightly bent) and then to groan down into our bodies I felt really silly, but others were doing it so I thought, 'What the heck'. He then made this beautiful sound into the microphone. I now know that it was a tone but then I had never heard such a sound before. I thought, 'Wow'—I could feel it right through my body. He then asked us to shape our mouths like a fish and copy his sound. It wasn't too hard really. And soon afterwards he got us to sing.

I tried out for the school choir when I was young and was told I couldn't sing, so that was that, I never tried again, but now with everybody around me singing it seemed so easy. As we all sang together I experienced something I've never felt before—there were tiny shivers running all over my body, I went really hot and then this feeling just went right through my body.

I had never felt so alive. I was glad I was not with Jenny as tears came into my eyes.

For the next week I couldn't get that feeling out of my mind. I told Jenny about it and she suggested I try to find out more about Chris. I didn't do anything about it, but then several months later I was driving to work and there was Chris talking on the radio. I stopped the car on the side of the road to listen and after a while he did a tone and even though it was through the radio I got some of that same feeling again. When I got to work I rang the radio station and got Chris's contact details. I enrolled in his next retreat, which was luckily in just a few weeks.

I hadn't ever been on a retreat before and was pretty nervous at the thought of going alone. However, once there it wasn't as daunting as I expected. Chris's work helped me to relax fairly quickly. I also found the other participants very friendly. There weren't many blokes there but I found it didn't matter. We all just talked together anyway. Once I started to relax I just decided to throw myself into the experience. I also enjoyed all the interesting conversations over meal times. It was all valuable.

As a result of the retreat I have now decided I want to do Chris's teacher training. Once I've done that I'll run a weekly toning group in our local community centre. I've now told the guys at work about what I am doing. I knew they'd find out about it anyway. They ragged me a bit about it at first but one of them is even talking about coming along to my group when I start it.

I've changed so much in the past few years and it is as though the retreat has just given me an extra push. I've decided I'd like to get out of the army now and do something different. I'm thinking of doing a massage course. Whatever I do, I know I want to work with people; however, one thing at a time. Since getting back from the retreat Jenny and I have decided to move in together. If somebody had told me five years ago that this would all be happening in my life I wouldn't have believed it. I've never felt so happy.

Retreats foster new understandings of Self

During my forties I have created time for retreats—going camping, attending five-day meditation courses, visiting an ashram for time out and participating in a variety of residential courses set in beautiful, natural locations. During these periods away from my everyday life I have consciously observed myself in these different settings. As a result I have arrived home with new practices for Self-nurturing and Self-understanding as well as new understandings about what else I might want to bring into my life. I am then able, over a period of time, to integrate many of them into my everyday living. Some of the essentials of a retreat for me would be:

- a location where I can enjoy and experience nature
- a place where I can have solitude when I want to
- others preparing my meals based around tasty, healthy, vegetarian, organic food
- if there is a facilitator, they are a person I can trust to create a space where I feel supported to experience my Self.

If you were to go on a retreat, what would be some of your requirements?

CHAPTER 28

men's groups

When men feel safe they will share at an enormous depth.

Owen Purse House, *Life Matters*, National Radio, 25 July 2002

AN UNFULFILLED NEED expressed by many of my interviewees was to be able to share with men friends in the way they had shared with me. There is often a difference between a man's world and a woman's world in relation to the support they will find in their relationships. Many women share openly with others their inner-most feelings, especially with women friends. This can be a rich place of support for a woman as she moves through the almost inevitable turbulent times of midlife transition. Women will even go to this place of intimate sharing with women they have just met. In contrast, men I interviewed said that they rarely had this intimate sharing with men, even with those they know well.

In their everyday conversation men tend to focus on their outer world, sometimes their own, but even more likely, the world beyond their own sphere. They feel comfortable discussing politics, sport, the economy, their share portfolio—but rarely, if ever, will they talk about their own inner world, even when there is obvious trauma happening in their life. A man can experience a traumatic event such as a parent's death, marriage break-up, children getting into trouble with the law, and not share this with others. He may even meet with a male friend and yet share little of this, or any of it in a feeling way.

At midlife, as a man's inner feminine is calling out for attention, his desire for meaningful, heartfelt interactions with others deepens. A man may fulfil this need by changing the way he relates to his wife, his lover or his daughter, but rarely will he fulfil this need through his relationships with other men. That is, unless he makes a conscious effort to create an environment where he feels comfortable doing so.

While writing this book I met a man who was part of a men's group. As he told me a little about the group I concluded it would be great to be able to write about it. I asked him if I could interview the men in it as part of my research. Subsequently, I made contact with each of them through email and asked if I could meet with them to hear about how they structured the group, why they joined the group in the first place, and what they got from it. Each said they would be happy to meet with me to share their experiences.

THE GROUP

The group came about after three members were sitting together at a school function. They had first met a year earlier through their children. Their wives were sitting elsewhere. They started talking about their children, and some of their feelings around their parenting. Towards the end of the evening they acknowledged how good it was to share with each other and somebody made a suggestion to start a 'fathers' group'. A couple of weeks later they met up at another school function and each expressed interest. Brian also said that he had two other friends who wanted to join.

A couple of them were trained in facilitation and group process skills. At the beginning of each session they have a 'catch up' time when each of them shares what has happened for them in the previous month. They have a structure to the two-hour meeting; however, when there is a 'pressing need' this will be put aside. For example, if there has been a major crisis for one of them during the month that needs attention this might take up much of the session. At times like this, there is a need to balance the needs of the individual with the needs of the group. In the group they have had formal discussion about the art of facilitation and having two people in the group already with these skills helps guide the process of the group, and the development of the others' facilitation skills.

From the beginning it was recognised the group was to be egalitarian—they wanted to avoid the power issues that so often affected men's gatherings. They each take it in turn to be the facilitator. The biggest issue was to commit to the monthly two-hour meeting. There were five of them and they noticed that often the best discussions happened when only three or four of them were present. The discussion was then more personal, rather than issues-based.

Each year they have a focus. This year the focus has been on the inner child. Other years they have focused on such issues as relationships with mother/father. As well as talking they use non-verbal methods, such as drawing, to explore various themes. Each of them sets a goal for the year. These are shared with the group and it is a given that the group will help, encourage and accompany them during the year in pursuing their goal. They also have activities outside their meeting time. They have had a father and son weekend. A benefit of this type of activity is that sons see their fathers relating to other men in an atypical, intimate way.

The biggest issue for the group was to sustain ongoing commitment. It was agreed that if there was trust and commitment, the process would flow. Developing trust had not been a problem and they thought this had been helped by the fact that each of them knew at least one other in the group. Another issue is whether they open up the group to other men. And recently they had also been talking about going out and doing something in the community. They found that an obvious desire after a time of self-exploration was to find a way to give to their local community. They had also started setting homework to be done between sessions. This assisted them to focus between meetings on their commitment to self-development.

Zac

I realised I had the desire to be part of such a group around the time I celebrated my fortieth birthday. I wanted to have a different relationship to men to those I had experienced in the past. I also had a desire to link with my own manhood. To have the focus as the fathers' group made it easier at the beginning, but soon it became obvious the group was about men and all sorts of relationships. The group gave me a place to explore myself, especially that part of me that had been suppressed. I can find in the other men a reflection of who I am. To get together with them in this way helps me integrate my sense of identity. It was a big shift to be with men in this way and not see them as competitors, but rather to look to them for support. The group helps me to get perspective on aspects of my life. As others share how they have approached something in their life, I find inspiration for my own concerns.

Phil

I have always enjoyed getting together with men to do all sorts of things. If men don't have an activity they don't get together. To start with, the reason we got together was to talk about fathering; however, soon we all realised there were many other things we wanted to talk about. It was a real challenge for me to break the habit and to share with other men, something I had only done with my female partner. Despite a lot of anxiety about joining the group, I did join because I trusted Zac, and he was the one who suggested it to me.

Often when the monthly meeting is coming up I'm thinking, 'Bloody hell, I haven't the time'. But once I sit down with the others I know I am in just the right place for me. I feel very connected to what is important to me and to other people in the group. And as a result I feel more connected to my partner and children. While there I feel that the clutter and the noise of everyday life is absent. I have time for me. I'd encourage other men to have a go. It has been the best thing I could do for myself at this time of my life. I now realise I am not alone. It has also helped me change my behaviour. There's nowhere else in life where I have this sort of contact with men. I have been to a therapeutic group, but this is different. Here we are all equal. We are all giving to each other, which is pretty radical for a group of men. It's different if there is a facilitator or therapist leading the group.

Brian

When I was approached by one of the others I jumped at the opportunity. I had been in a men's group before and was looking again for that level of intimacy. This group was specifically all fathers and originally there was a focus on the initiation of fatherhood. For me the thought of intimacy with other men—to share stories, to speak with meaning and from the heart about problems and issues such as how you raise your children, what your father was like, and how you cope with your wife—was both scary and compelling.

For many years I have searched for a 'good father'. Since joining the group four years ago this need has become less. The group is like 'mother's milk' to me. I feel very nurtured there. I have also found that my way of relating outside the group has changed. When at social gatherings I now have a tendency to talk to other men in a more open way. If they are not comfortable with it, I find they just move away. I now have little tolerance for conversations where there is just discussion about generalities.

Michel

I didn't want to come to the group, but Brian was enthusiastic about it and I couldn't think of a good reason to say no. But now I am very clear that I get a lot from it. The companionship has meant a lot to me. I don't have any other men in my life I could talk to like this. When my marriage broke up six months ago I don't think I would have had anyone else to talk to. After telling the guys here about it, it was easier for me to tell people at work. So there is a flow-on effect.

When I first came to the group it reminded me of something I hadn't experienced since I was a kid. I had two good friends I'd walk home from school with. We'd stop at my front gate and talk for hours about our feelings. This all stopped when I was a teenager. So it's like when I was a kid. I can be honest. The group has a conscious focus on integrity and a spirit of generosity where we give others praise for their effort. I don't think it is always easy for me to be generous in my praise.

DEVELOPING INTIMATE RELATIONSHIPS WITH OTHER MEN

If you felt the need, would you consider making a conscious effort to develop more intimate relationships with men? It doesn't have to be through a men's group. One of my interviewees, Ross, found that creating such a relationship in his life happened by chance. However, once seeing the opportunity for such a relationship, he seized it. This is what he told me.

Ross

I benefited from forming a confidential and candid relationship with one of my partners at work. It was almost by accident It started about fifteen years ago, at the age of 40. Quite by chance, when I made an unguarded comment to him he tentatively started opening up to me about a similar concern. Since then we have both greatly enjoyed and benefited from our 'chats'. He is the only person who I share secrets with that I don't share with my wife. I can sometimes feel a bit guilty about this. It is such a relief and release though because often we share similar concerns. He doesn't always agree with me. Sometimes he makes me realise I do have a problem.

I am not suggesting that the only way to bring intimate, male relationships into your life is by joining a men's group. Like Ross, you might be able to create this through encounters in your everyday life. In Ross's words, 'I know a men's group can be great, but the same effect can arise from a one-to-one relationship with a work colleague or friend if the trust and chemistry is right'. However, if you did want to consider attending a men's group contact your local men's health organisation for information about men's groups in your area or search the Internet for organisations such as Mensline (details in Bibliography).

PART 7

The river is there for the rest of your life

CHAPTER 29

the hero returns to bestow boons on his fellow man

Having spent much if not all our time looking after ourselves (and if we are parents, after our children) many of us find ourselves wanting to help others. Working in an orphanage etc. is not what we associate with a midlife crisis. But it is precisely such acts of service to other human beings, other creatures, or the planet itself that spontaneously emerge in the quest for wholeness. It connects us to a world beyond ourselves. It places our own life in perspective. It enables us to have an impact, to make a difference. It allows us to learn what only service can teach.

M. Scott Peck, *Further Along the Road Less Travelled*

IN JOSEPH CAMPBELL'S study of world mythology, *The Hero With a Thousand Faces*, the questing hero's journey is often a very lonely one. However, at journey's end, there is the reward of a sense of true connection with oneself, with others, and with the world at large, and an understanding of one's destiny; all enabling the hero to bestow boons on his fellow man.

It is now time to consider where you are on this hero's journey. You have listened to other men's stories and now connected with your own. As we now review some of the lessons encountered along the path of midlife transition, I encourage you to notice where your energy is drawn, for this is an indication of where you need to focus next in your own midlife journey.

TEN TRAVEL TIPS FOR MIDLIFE TRANSITION

At the beginning of midlife transition you start to realise that much in life is paradoxical. As you let go of illusions from the first half of your life, you begin to question and you learn that there are many different ways of looking at your Self and your world. You begin to learn lessons very different from those learnt in the first half of life.

One

You grew up learning that the way to make progress in life was to know and develop those parts of you that are valued by society. This helped you create a solid foundation for earning a living, forming a network of relationships and creating a place for yourself in the world. Now you have learnt that to continue your psychological growth at midlife, you need to get to know the side you have learnt to hide away from yourself and others. You have to go on a hero's journey.

Two

For some this heroic journey is taken with some ease, for others much less so. In particular, for those neglected and abused when young, midlife transition can be a very challenging time. A man's personality type can also affect the ease with which he can bring into his life the feeling aspect that is so vital for this journey.

Three

As a young boy you were encouraged to believe that happiness would come through striving for material gain and outer success. Now you have learnt that an ongoing prime focus on your outer, material world at midlife leads to feelings of emptiness. Whether it be through such happenings as illness, depression or an inner voice telling you to do so, at midlife transition you let go of a predominant focus on the external world, and give this time to your spiritual life. You still attend to everyday matters; however, you now know that for a sense of balance and wellbeing you need to make time for your spiritual Self, preferably daily.

Four

When young you took for granted your good health. Now you have learnt you need to nurture yourself. You have to nurture your body on every level—physically, emotionally, intellectually and spiritually—as this supports you as you navigate the turbulence of midlife. You have learnt that your psyche is continually sending you messages from your unconscious.

If you don't take notice of these messages at midlife they get louder and louder. Illness at midlife is often a warning sign that there is something in your inner world you need to attend to. You can go to the gym, eat well and do all you are told to on a physical level and still suffer a major illness. So whereas when young you were conditioned to not notice your body's signals, now you have learnt to view illness as a sign that personal work needs to be done. You even come to view illness as a gift as it guides you towards the river of your life.

Five

In the first half of life you learnt to avoid those things you feared. Now you understand your fears will lead you to exactly the things you need to give time and attention for your own development. You learn to notice your fears, navigate yourself towards them, and as you do you open your Self and your life up to a much fuller reality. You are an adult now. You trust you can create your own security within yourself.

Six

Whereas in the first half of life you were encouraged to ignore many of your feelings now you have learnt it is important to 'befriend yourself' and notice and experience all of them. For example, it is important to experience all the sad feelings that are inevitable as you grieve for the passing of the first part of your life and for all that you now know will never be.

Seven

You have learnt that it is important at midlife to find a way to connect to your own story. As you connect with your own story, memories come flooding back. This remembering encourages you to reclaim parts of your Self repressed long ago. As you reconnect with the sad and wounded boy within, you also experience all the joy and wonder of your inner child.

Eight

In the first half of life you learnt not to share your feelings of vulner-ability with men. As you start to experience all your memories and emotions you realise how isolated you are. Now you wonder if other men feel the same way. Finally you have the courage to reach out to share—perhaps to a male counsellor, a male friend or with men in a workshop or men's group. You discover that it can be okay to talk this way to men. You can trust them. In the right setting you are listened to. This helps you feel validated.

It is wonderful to share in this way. As you practise expressing your feelings to other men it becomes easier. The more you do it, the more you realise that there are many men out there who want to share their feelings.

Nine

You have learnt that as you enjoy an intimate relationship with your-self, your ability to enjoy a deep, emotional connection with both men and women grows. You have also learnt that your expression of your own sexuality changes at midlife and these changes lead to increasing intimacy with your partner.

Ten

In the first half of life you were told that being self-centred was being selfish. Now you have learnt that as you accept and have compassion for all of your Self, you are able to show this same attitude to others. You now know that being self-centred enables you to give out to others from a place deep within yourself. You now look within to find what will give you personal satisfaction. You gradually follow a call to your vocation.

WHERE ARE YOU ON YOUR MIDLIFE JOURNEY?

If you focus on how you are living your life right now and look at the travel tips above, how do you think you are faring? If you are in your mid to late forties or early fifties, do you feel you have successfully negotiated midlife transition? If yes, you may have already moved on to the next stage—middle adulthood.

In *The Seasons of a Man's Life*, Daniel Levinson suggests that middle adulthood extends from 45 years to 60 years. He describes the tasks necessary to enter middle adulthood as to make crucial choices, give the choices meaning and commitment, and build a life structure around them. He found that most men were not ready by the age of 45 to create this new life structure.

Levinson points out that a man needed more time to establish the choices around which a new life structure can be built. He also points out that a man may never accomplish this task.

In short, an integrated structure may emerge early or late in
entering Middle Adulthood, or not at all. A man stays in this
period, however, as long as his predominant developmental
task is to create a satisfactory structure. (p. 279)

You can go back at a later time to do developmental work missed
out on at an earlier stage of life. No matter what your age, you can
now work to make crucial choices that will create a new life structure
which suits the person you truly are. So how might this time of
moving on to middle adulthood unfold for a man? According to
Daniel Levinson:

The end of the Midlife Transition, like all shifts from one
period to the next, is marked by a series of changes rather
than one dramatic event. It may be evident only as a man
looks back a few years later that he was in fact committing
himself to the choices around which a new life structure
took shape. (p. 61)

As I write this last chapter Michael is 53 years old. He is now at
the stage where he can look back at this time of making crucial
choices, giving them meaning, committing to them, and building a
life structure around them. Parts of the story you have heard from
Michael before; however, this time, as he speaks eighteen months
after our initial interview, it is easier for him to see how the crucial
choices he made at midlife have brought him to where he is now.
These choices enabled him to minimise the gap between his core
values and how they are reflected in the way he now chooses to
live. As he enters middle adulthood he believes he has created a life
structure that enables him to do exactly what he was destined to do.
This is what he has to say about this time.

Michael

A whole range of changes took place in my life around the age of
43 when I felt a clear need to leave the business world. I also knew

this would mean my marriage would break apart. However, I knew I had to take this step of leaving the business world, simplifying my life, giving myself time to explore things in life I had never before had time to. I followed up on a long-term desire to do volunteer work and within four weeks of leaving my management position I was working locally as a volunteer. I found this a very humbling experience. I also explored my artistic interests and started a counselling course. I really enjoyed all of this and it helped me open up to a new dimension in me.

While I was doing all this exploring often I was wondering what I should be doing next in my life. At times I felt a real urgency to have another professional focus for my life. I followed a few leads here and there but they didn't go anywhere. Then I was approached to take on the position of general manager at the place where I had been doing volunteer work. I was reluctant to take it up, but after the third approach I decided to accept as I could see there was a need there. I was very clear that whatever I was doing there I wouldn't compromise my values. Given that it was a not-for-profit organisation I felt a comfort taking up the role. But as the years went by I became increasingly disinterested and bored with management, something I had been doing for so long. There came a time after five years in the job that it became clear I had to make a change.

For the last ten years I've spent three to five days around New Year's Day taking myself through a review process. I review the previous twelve months, seeing what I want to let go of, what I want to carry forward into the next year, and what other things I want to bring into my life in the following twelve months. Part of this process is also a thorough review of my basic values. During these five days I spend a lot of time in a meditative space, as well as writing.

When I did this review at the age of 50 it became very clear to me that my heart was calling me to let go of the management side altogether and to pursue a career in counselling. I had already completed a qualification in counselling and knew that I enjoyed the work. At the end of this review time I made a decision to make this fundamental career change in the following twelve months. Shortly after this I told my workplace of my plan. I said I would resign my role of general manager before the end of the year and wanted to pursue a role as counsellor, preferably within the organisation, or if this was not possible I would pursue it elsewhere.

During that year I resigned as general manager before I had anything else lined up. Eventually they offered me the opportunity to work as a counsellor. There wasn't any budget allocation for this role so I offered to use up my five months of accumulated leave and for the first year to work for very little money while I established the position. So within twelve months of having done the review and made the decision to change I had implemented it all.

The first year in my new role as a counsellor was a particularly challenging and difficult experience. In my professional management role I had a lot of expertise, a good track record and a lot of confidence. My ego got bruised quite a lot during this year as I gained confidence in myself and gained the confidence of the organisation that I could perform in this new role. I also needed to gain the support of my fellow staff members because before I was in a role of formal authority as general manager whereas now in my apprentice role I was one of them. After the first year in my new role I also decided to enrol in another counselling course to get a formal tertiary qualification in my new field as my business-related qualifications didn't count for anything anymore.

Now, at the end of my second year of my new career I feel very confident and competent in what I am doing. I am well accepted in the organisation. I get a lot of positive feedback from clients and I feel totally fulfilled in what I am doing to an extent I have never been fulfilled before in my life. Now exactly ten years since leaving my business management role in a large company it feels that the job of general manager for a not-for-profit organisation was a stepping stone for letting go of the management career leading me eventually to a totally new orientation in line with my values and potential.

In parallel with these changes in my professional life, there have been equally profound changes in my major relationship. As indicated before, when I left my management job, my marriage of about twenty years came to an end. There was total separation and splitting up of the assets. Then after about nine months we re-established our marriage based on very different arrangements compared to before. We continued to live in separate houses, we had separate bank accounts and we spent time with each other when we both felt like doing so—usually a day or so a week. In the following seven years we explored many different ways of being a couple—sometimes living together and sometimes not—but with total fidelity to our relationship. Finally, at exactly the time I had resigned as the general manager it also became clear that we had reached the end of the road we could travel together and we finally separated and subsequently divorced. During this same seven years the children, who were in their early twenties, were developing their own lives, sometimes living with me and sometimes living with their mother.

The time following the separation was a difficult time of letting go and grieving for the then 27-year marriage but it also felt deeply right having taken the step to separate. And I was determined for quite some time to not rush into another relationship. There came a time when I started to explore other relationships, realising at the same time a certain fear of allowing myself to be intimate. I was prepared to explore physical intimacy but finally realised I had a fear around emotional intimacy. I felt quite attracted during this exploration phase to younger women—by about ten years—but I eventually felt strongly attracted to a woman of a similar developmental stage of life to me—somebody who had already been through this time of turbulence of midlife transition. One year into this relationship I feel very fulfilled, more fulfilled than I've ever felt in my life.

My children are now well in to their twenties and have fairly well established their own lives and so there is less and less demand from them in a material way, although we are clearly still part of each other's lives. So overall it is a most fulfilling and rich time of life.

STAYING CENTRED ON THE RIVER OF YOUR LIFE

As Michael moved into middle adulthood he made some crucial choices in both his work and his primary relationship. After daily inner work, these choices came from an increasing understanding of what was most meaningful to him. I can think of many other men at a similar stage of life who have made crucial choices. Simon sold his business and now directs much of his energy into creating partnerships between business and Aboriginal communities. Robert left his corporate life and now has his own business mentoring others, including the mentoring of younger people which he does on a voluntary basis. Rodney started a business publishing books with a heart-centred, personal growth focus. Carl and his wife moved to Africa, and now run an orphanage there for children whose parents are victims of the AIDS virus. And many others make crucial choices as they finally leave long-term careers and relationships. These are all outer changes, and whether or not they bring personal fulfilment to an individual will depend on the inner work done to reach that choice. Other men will do the inner work, and as a result approach their life differently, although without the need to make significant outer changes.

As you come to the end of *Men Navigating Midlife* I encourage you now to take time to look within and ask yourself the following questions:

- Where am I on my midlife journey?
- If I am still journeying midlife transition what do I need to commit to now in order to continue this journey?
- If I am in middle adulthood, what crucial choices have I made as I entered this stage of life?
- Have these choices enabled me to create a life structure for the second half of my life where I have the opportunity to experience my uniqueness, my full potential, my destiny?
- If not, what other crucial choices do I need to consider?

Once you start making crucial choices based on Self-understanding, life is more fulfilling. This fulfilment comes from increasingly living a life where there is congruence between the person you know you are inside, and the life you are creating for yourself. You still experience ups and downs, but by now you accept that these times are a normal, and in fact an important part of life, as they navigate you towards the personal work you continue to do to stay centred on the river of your life.

Whether you are navigating midlife transition or middle adulthood, you continue the work of noticing your Self, healing your wounds, and creating a life that allows you to express the unique individual you are. You now know that there is no map anyone else can give you to guide you down the river of your life. Your map is the moment-by-moment noticing of your Self and your experiences; this moment-by-moment noticing leads you to your destiny; fulfilling your destiny allows you to bestow boons upon your fellow man.

bibliography

Australian Financial Review, 'Compassion when lives are on the line', by Jill Margo, 11 April 2002, p. 59

Badinter, E., 1997, *XY: De l'identite Masculine*, Columbia University Press

Bearman, S., 2000, 'Why Men Are So Obsessed With Sex', in Kay, Nagle & Gould, *Male Lust*, Harrington Park Press, New York

Bell, H., *All About Love: New Visions*, William Morrow, New York

Bly, R., 1992, *Iron John*, Vintage Books, Random House, New York

Bradshaw, J., 1988, *Healing the Shame That Binds You*, Health Communications Inc., Florida

Brennan, A. & Brewi, J., 1991, *Mid-Life: Psychological and Spiritual Perspectives*, The Crossroad Publishing Co., New York

——1999, *Midlife Spirituality and Jungian Archetypes*, Nicholas-Hays, York Beach, ME

Bridges, W., 1991, *Managing Transitions*, Addison-Wesley, Reading, MASS

Campbell, J., 1970, *The Hero with a Thousand Faces*, World Publishing Company, New York

Cassou, M., 2001, *Point Zero: Creativity Without Limits*, Penguin Putnam Inc, New York

Chodron, P., 1997, *When Things Fall Apart*, Shambhala Publications Inc., Boston

Corlett, E. & Millner, N., 1993, *Navigating Midlife*, Consulting Psychologists Press, Palo Alto, CA

Costello, T., 1999, *Tips From a Travelling Soul Searcher*, Allen & Unwin, Sydney

Covey, S., 1989, *The Seven Habits of Highly Effective People*, The Business Library, Melbourne

Furth, G., 2002, *The Secret World of Drawings*, Inner City Books, Toronto

Frost, R., 1973, *Robert Frost: Selected Poems*, Penguin Books, Melbourne

Gawler, Dr I., 2000, *Meditation Pure and Simple*, Hill of Content, Melbourne

Gerzon, M., 1992, *Listening to Midlife: Turning Your Crisis Into a Quest*, Shambhala Publications Inc., Boston

Hollis, J.,1993, *The Middle Passage: From Misery To Meaning In Midlife*, Inner City Books, Toronto

Jelinek, Prof G., 2000, *Taking Control of Multiple Sclerosis*, Hyland House Publishing, Melbourne

Johnson, R., 1983, *We*, Harper & Row, San Francisco

——1991, *Owning Your Own Shadow*, Harper San Francisco, San Francisco

Jung, Carl G., 1933, *Modern Man In Search Of A Soul*, Harcourt-Brace, New York

——1956, *Two Essays on Analytical Psychology*, 2nd ed., translated by R. F. C. Hull, Meridian Books, New York

——1971, *Psychological Types*, Princeton University Press, Princeton, NJ

——1983, *Memories, Dreams and Reflections*, edited by Aniela Jaffe, translated by Richard and Clara Winston, Vintage Books, New York

——1990, *Man And His Symbols*, Penguin, London

Kaplan, R. E., Drath, W. H. & Kofodimos, J. R., 1991, *Beyond Ambition: How Driven Managers Can Lead Better and Live Better*, Jossey Bess, San Francisco

Kay, K., Nagle, J. & Gould, B., 2000, *Male Lust: Pleasure, Power and Transformation*, Harrington Park Press, New York

Keen, S., 1991, *Fire In the Belly*, Bantam Books, New York

Kubler-Ross, E., 1970, *On Death and Dying*, Tavistock Publications Ltd, London

Leunig, Michael, 1993, *Common Prayer Collection*, Collins Dove, Melbourne

'Life Matters', interview by Geraldine Dougue with Owen Purse House, broadcast 25 July 2002, ABC Radio National

Levinson, D., 1978, *The Seasons of a Man's Life*, Ballantine Books, New York

Mensline: phone 1300 78 99 78 within Australia; email talkitover@ menslineaus.org.au; website www.menslineaus.org.au

Moore, T., 1992, *Care of the Soul*, Harper Collins, New York

Myers, I. with Myers, P. 1990, *Gifts Differing*, Consulting Psychologists Press, Palo Alto, CA

Nelson Bolles, R., 1993, *What Color is Your Parachute?*, Ten Speed Press, California

O'Connor, Dr P., 1981, *Understanding the Mid-Life Crisis*, Sun Books Pty Ltd, Melbourne

——1988, *Understanding Jung*, Reed Books, Melbourne

O' Donohue, J., 1997, *Anam Cara—Spiritual Wisdom from the Celtic World*, Bantam Press, Great Britain

——1999, *Eternal Echoes: Celtic Reflections on Our Yearning to Belong*, HarperCollins Publishers Inc., New York

Oliver, M., 1986, *Dream Work*, Grove/Atlantic Inc., Berkeley, CA

Paul, S. & Collins, G., 1990, *Illuminations: Visions for Change, Growth and Self-Acceptance*, HarperCollins Publishers, New York

Sardello, R., 1999, *Freeing the Soul from Fear*, The Berkeley Publishing Group, New York

Schnark, D., 1997, *Passionate Marriage*, Scribe Publications, Melbourne

Sheehy, G., 1996, *New Passages*, HarperCollins Publishers, Great Britain

——1998, *Passages for Men*, Simon & Schuster, Sydney

——1981, *Pathfinders: Overcoming the Crisis of Adult Life and Finding Your Own Path to Well-Being*, William Morrow, New York

Scott Peck, Dr M., 1993, *Further Along the Road Less Travelled*, Simon & Schuster, New York

Stein, M., 1983, *In Midlife: A Jungian Perspective*, Spring Publications, Dallas

Stone, Dr H., 1989, *Embracing Heaven and Earth*, Delos Inc., California

Suzuki, D. & Knudtson, P., 1992, *Wisdom of the Elders*, Allen & Unwin, Sydney

Vaillant, G., 2002, *Ageing Well: Surprising Guideposts to a Happier Life from the Harvard Study of Adult Development*, Scribe Publications, New York

Wordsworth, W., 2002, *Lyrical Ballads and Related Writings*, Houghton Mifflin & Co

index